The Covenant Between the King of Devils and Death

JAMES DE ROUSSEAU

Order this book online at www.trafford.com
or email orders@trafford.com

Most Trafford titles are also available at major online book retailers.

Printed in the United States of America.

ISBN: 978-1-4669-8385-4 (sc)
ISBN: 978-1-4669-8384-7 (e)

Trafford rev. 05/15/2013

Trafford www.trafford.com
PUBLISHING®

North America & international
toll-free: 1 888 232 4444 (USA & Canada)
phone: 250 383 6864 ♦ fax: 812 355 4082

EPISODE 1

THE POWER OF THE WORD

The Eternal Spirit is a self created Element in the light with the power of the WORD to create Sprits like Himself in the light by the WORD to maintain peace and harmony in the universe with power to eliminate Death if he trespass in His worlds in the light.

The Eternal Spirit in the light, ruler of all worlds in the light from the highest world to the world Armageddon as the boundary between light and darkness.

Death is a spirit from the element of the dark worlds the ruler of all worlds in the dark from Armageddon and worlds beneath the earth.

Under the covenant for peace and harmony in the universe, Death should not trespass in worlds in the light.

There was peace and harmony in the universe for millions of years, the Eternal took his rest and all worlds in the light were in darkness while he took his rest.

DEATH

Death was asleep in the lower region in Armageddon, he heard a voice; 'You need help to populate the worlds above' Death said; 'how can it be done? 'I am alone living in this chamber in Armageddon.' Death woke up and was disturbed from sleep.

Death fell asleep again and was seduced by a female coming out of his spirit, when he woke up he saw the spirit sitting next to him. She said; 'I am the spirit who came from you to help you populate the worlds.' She said; 'Death, if you fuck me I'll make a spirit and all spirits who pass on your seed shall be from the same element as you to live for Death.

Death fucked her and she gave birth to a spirit, she asked Death what is his name? Death replied; 'I will call him Devil' Death said 'When you go above, Devil shall be your king to populate devils with you for Death.

THE COVENANT BETWEEN KING DEVIL AND DEATH

The time came for Devil and his mother to go to the worlds above. Death said to the mother of Devil; ill make a covenant with you and your King. Devil, you shall have my power and strength to pass on my seed and make devils to populate all worlds in the dark with devils, but the day any devil disturbs the peace and harmony and go in the worlds in the light, they will contaminate the worlds with disease of Death, an every devil will return to me in Armageddon for ever.'

Death said to the mother of Devil, you shall be the Queen of devils when you are above, I have been living alone all my life and have never been in the worlds above, because there is a Spirit that keeps an eye for peace in the universe, if I went above, the spirit would set Armageddon on fire.' Death said to devil, I am afraid of fire, it's your mother who wants to populate devils with you to pass on my seed to make devils to live above.

Death said, the Spirit of light keep his eye on peace and harmony in the universe, give this Spirit in the light no reason to rule all worlds above for ever to have the victory over Death. So with all my power, rule the worlds in the dark with your Queen mother and populate the worlds with devils like yourself, if any devil come between you and your mother, cast them in the hole of Armageddon to live with me for ever!'

Death said, 'Devil, you and your Queen mother are bound by this covenant to live above for Death, be fruitful, multiply devils in all worlds in the dark as king to have dominion, any devil that has no faith with your authority return them to me.'

Devil said', With your power, I will rule as a mighty King when I populate devils and will send disobedient devils to you as a peace offering, according to the covenant with you and my Queen Mother.'

THE KING OF DEVILS AND QUEEN MOTHER

The King of devils and his Queen mother left Armageddon for the ancient worlds in the dark, she gave birth to a devil for her king. The king of devils said 'My Queen, what name shall you call him? She said 'Now I have a prince from the seed of Death, I will name him Satan.

Many generations later, the worlds in the dark were populated with multitude of devils living in poverty and fighting each other for food. Every devil who was the strongest in their world became a king. The King of all devils came in his palace and saw Satan fucking his Queen. The King shouted 'Mother fucker, what are you doing? Satan said; 'If I am a mother fucker, you are a mother fucker too! She is my mother just like you, they began to fight for the Queen, the king threw him outside and said 'Next time, I'll throw you in the pit for Death to punish you. Satan returned to his world with hate for the mighty King.

The Queen of devils began to cry. Oh my King, it's my fault, Satan seduced me, he said he wanted me to make a devil to look like him. The king said 'you've been pregnant making devils for me since Death sent us above to populate the worlds with devils, all devils look alike, passing on the seed of Death and that includes Satan, your prince. You are always complaining, you want something better in the worlds, I begin to think I can't satisfy you, is Satan better than me?' The Queen Mother replied, no my king, the King said you have allowed Satan to corrupt you to satisfy his lust, he is envious of my power.'

The King became angry and jealous, he began to swear 'You mother fucker, you are never satisfied, the King began to beat her up, she began to cry, Oh my king have mercy on me, Satan seduced me. The king shouted, 'So your prince thinks he is better than me?' 'He pushed her away she fell and cried loudly help! Some devils rushed inside, the King said, take the queen to the dungeon and lock her up, she cried

'If you put me in the dungeon, I'm no more your queen. The King shouted 'You will remain there until you return to Death. The queen cried 'Ok king, have mercy. From that time onwards, the King of devils became cruel to other devils.

THE QUEEN OF DEVILS

The Queen stopped crying and accepted her fate to live in the dungeon until she returned to Death. She began to live in hope. The Queen began to make enchantment for the Spirit of light to come and let her out. She began saying 'Oh Spirit of light, I invoke thee, I want your help, come into my world and do what is not yet done by the king of devils for peace and harmony in the worlds, my King has no mercy, he has became cruel to me. Instruct me O spirit of Light I will do what you want, come and illuminate the worlds in the dark from the highest of worlds and I'll be satisfied for eternity.

Oh Spirit, from the highest heaven, Oh come and cast out the king and Satan for seducing the mother of devil, She began to cry day after day making enchantments,' Oh Spirit of Light come and take revenge for me, I'm in this miserable dungeon crying to you for help.

'Oh Spirit of Light let my sorrow turn to joy in your worlds with Spirits from your Element with goodly shape to populate all worlds, She began to cry, Oh Spirit in the light, I'm in this miserable place by the King, do the same to him and return him to Death to suffer like I am suffering in this dungeon.'

The Queen began to be hungry and in pain crying loud for the king to let her out, she was in fear the king would never let her out of the dungeon as long as Satan lived in the world. She became desperate and in fear of returning to Death.

Day after day the Queen cried and hoped the Eternal Spirit would come to remove her from the dungeon, she cried, 'I'm hungry, I'm suffering in pain every day. My king will not let me out, my only hope oh Spirit of Light is you, come and set me free from this dungeon.

THE QUEEN HAD A VISION

The Queen fell asleep, the Eternal Spirit in the Light gave the Queen of devils a vision, when she saw the Eternal Spirit in the light, She tried to speak and could not and was afraid, the Eternal spirit said, 'You asked me to come in this dungeon to set you free, your devils have trespassed in my worlds while I took my rest, I Live in the highest of my worlds. I created myself with the WORD and if I say the WORD, all devils will return to Death, because Death has broken the covenant of peace in the universe by making devil to populate my worlds. The devils are fighting each other and this is not acceptable for peace and harmony.'

The queen said, 'Oh Eternal Spirit, how did you create yourself with the WORD? I am a spirit from Death, can you remove me from this miserable place to live with you? I will not stray from you. The Holy ETERNAL Spirit in the Light did not answer, an the vision vanished.

The Queen; Fell asleep again and had another vision. I saw the Sprit in the Light, I looked at him, he looked at me. He held my hands and I and the Eternal Spirit was flying all over the worlds. When we got to the world earth, he said it's my paradise. I saw creatures of all kinds and beasts, I saw fields, mountains, water falls, with rivers flowing water to the sea, saw trees with fruit that looked succulent, I had much desire to eat flesh of the beasts and creatures and the fruit on earth. When I woke up, I realised it was another vision and wondered if the Holy Spirit was showing me the new world earth.

Queen; 'I began to rejoice and suddenly I became afraid what my king would do to me for contacting the Holy Spirit in the Light to remove Him and devils back to Armageddon to Death. I fell on my knees trembling and was in fear my King would return me to Death for asking the Eternal Spirit to come and remove devils from His worlds we occupy.'

The Eternal Spirit thundered in my ear, I am a creator and will create all you saw on earth. The earth is my paradise, every tree that you saw with fruit, I created and also the creatures and beasts with flesh, if any devil come in paradise to make a god in flesh with my creation, my CHRIST who I will create will claim your half of the universe for trespass in paradise to make a god, so warn all devils not to come to earth to make gods to live to Death.'

Queen; 'I was in fear after this vision, what the CHRIST of Eternal will do to devils if they went to earth to make gods in flesh. I said, Eternal Spirit, you have given me a vision of what will take place before it happens to me and all devils.'

Queen; 'O Eternal Spirit, I am locked in this dungeon, I have no devil at hand to share these visions with, the future of your worlds. 'I am in solitude, O Eternal waiting to return to Death, how can I tell devils not to go to earth to make gods with your creation. The Eternal thundered in my ear, every god that is born from the seed of devils with my creation will be your spirits and Death. When I will create my CHRIST he will create his Elijah with the WORD, to remove every devil if they made a god on earth.

Queen said; O Eternal be patient with me as I speak, you took me to earth, you call your paradise and made me see trees and fruits and all kinds of creatures and beasts which would delight all devils, which is larking in the worlds in the dark'. 'If any devil made a god with your creation, there spirits will be from the seed of devils I've made with my King with Death. I am not satisfied with my King. How can any god satisfy me? They will have fellow ship with devils passing on the seed of devils to make gods for Death.

The Eternal thundered while you are held in captivity in the dungeon, you and all devils have a choice for peace, by returning to Death in Armageddon, where you came from. 'I am self sufficient and in possession of happiness. I am alone for eternity, no devil in the universe is like me or equal to hold a conversation. I create spirits by the WORD. To live in my worlds, you are inferior to any spirit I will create.'

Queen; said, O Eternal Spirit how can I be a Spirit in the Light like you, to know your ways. I came from death and my first devil is my

King, he is not intelligent like you, he is cruel and not merciful to me. My king put fear in the devils to return them to Death they have not seen, neither any devil my king has thrown in the hole of Armageddon to Death has ever returned. Every devil lives in fear to return Death for punishment, O Eternal, you made me see clearly a better universe with worlds from earth to the highest of worlds for your creation.'

Queen said; O Holy Eternal, could you give me a Spirit to be like you, to converse and populate Spirits in the light like you. I know I have many faults, because I came from Death, also my king has many faults, passing on the seed of Death to make devils.'

Queen said, Eternal, before your create your CHRIST, give me a Spirit in the light to abide with me instead of a god who will do the same as devils to pass on the seed of death to make spirits for Death.

The Eternal said; when I create my CHRIST, He will create the Son you ask for, and will manifest in the image for Salvation by the WORD to be with the WORD and do his Holy work when CHRIST is on the throne of the worlds. It is important, Queen of devils, to understand the difference between Spirits of creation and spirits from the seed of devils of Death while you are in this dungeon by your King.

The Eternal said; These visions you are having while you are in the dungeon is to show you all I have in mind, and for you to know that what I will do next in the universe will please thee for peace and harmony on all worlds forever after the final judgement in kingdoms on earth.

Queen; 'I closed my eyes in deep sleep like Death, I woke up and saw before me, the Eternal Spirit in the light, he stood and healed my wounds by the king of devils. I woke up to find it was a vision of all I desired with the Eternal Spirit in the light, he showed me all the things that will happen on earth. I was overjoyed when I saw in the vision a woman coming out of a man, the same way I came out from Death from the element of darkness.'

Queen; 'I said O' Eternal, I saw the man you created and a woman coming out of his body, O Eternal thou art a creator, you have created the most beautiful woman in the world on earth. I am inferior to her and shall no more call myself the Queen of the worlds, but goddess to god's that will be born from the seed of devils and hope your CHRIST will rule the universe.'

The Eternal said; When I will create my CHRIST, his Queen will be called Zion.

Queen said; 'Thanks for letting me know the name Zion who will be the Queen of the universe after I return to Death so she can rule with Spirits with ever lasting life in the worlds in the light.

THE KING OF DEVILS DEBATE IN THE SYNAGOGUE

The King of devils invited the King of devils from other worlds to the synagogue of devils for a meeting, when all the Kings were together, the King of all devils said I had a dream.

Death said; The Spirit in the light is coming in his worlds, to remove all devils in his worlds for trespass in his worlds. He can't sleep. He is in fear of what the Eternal Spirit will do to him and devils in his worlds.

Death said; Before he made my queen mother there was peace and harmony without devils in the worlds, A covenant was made for peace and harmony with the Sprit in the Light and he could sleep forever.' Devils have violated the peace covenant.

Death said; All the sins of devils have come against him and it was a sin to make a devil to be the mother of devils. He can hear my queen crying in the dungeon, she is suffering like him in Armageddon. All devils are corrupt, there is no peace they fight each other and have no faith in their kings. Death wants all devils to return to him to the last born from his seed for peace in the worlds. The Eternal Spirit is coming to return every devil from his worlds, back to him in Armageddon for trespassing in forbidden worlds. I should warn all devils before Eternal Spirit come to put his worlds in order'

The King of devils said; Satan Death is angry with you, it's because of your envy, my queen is in the dungeon, he continued to tell the Kings of his dream.

Death said; 'My cruelty to my Queen Mother has activated change for peace by the Eternal Spirit which I and all devils do not know'

The king of devils said to the Kings 'I asked you kings from other worlds to come to this meeting, as this dream concerns all devils in the worlds, this Spirit that is coming will pursue every devil until they return to Death.

A devil said king of devils, if this Spirit is on the highest world, how can you catch him? No devil has ever been there, there is much mystery attached to the highest world. King, when you were with Death did he tell you about the highest world?'

The king of devils said; 'Death kept it a secret. He said he was afraid of fire that is why he lived in the chamber of Armageddon.'

Another devil said; O Almighty king, if you went to the highest world, you would have the advantage to see all worlds, use your power an capture him for Death!

Another devil said;' Almighty king, let us set a trap for him from the highest world and teach him never to show his face in the world for ever.'

A giant devil said; 'Almighty king, I have fought giant devils to be a king of my world, so we have to keep watch for this mystery spirit. The almighty king said;' I am liaising to all options available so we can continue to live in his worlds.

Another devil said; 'O mighty king, if this mystery spirit is not from Death, he can't be a devil. He can't hide if he came in my world, I and my devils will see who he is and we will offer him to Death as a peace offering'

The giant said 'Almighty king, it looks as if this strange spirit has put fear on devils more than Death.'

Another devil said;' Almighty king, I had to fight devils to be a king to rule my world, if this spirit come in my world, my devils will chastise him before we send him to Death.

Satan said;' Almighty King, I am your prince with your queen, who is also my mother, if this Spirit came in my world, my devils will chastise him, he will wish he never came in my world. I am the prince of Death and this mystery spirit will do all I say then send him Death.

Almighty king, you are the strongest of all devils and have the power of Death to rule all worlds, if the Eternal Spirit came, he would want to make himself equal with you. He will take our worlds and say its justified to send you and all devils back to Death for trespassing in His world an your offence and cruelty to my queen mother.

Another devil said;' Almighty King, you are not the only king that came from our queen from Death. We are all brothers gathered in council, if this Spirit took residence in the highest world, no devil will have peace in their worlds. He will want to populate Spirits to have possession in all the worlds. What can you do? This Spirit is the enemy

Satan said; king of devils; I hope to be a mighty king like you one day, so let us who are with you in council, make an oath to capture this ETERNAL in the light so all devils in future generations can do the same to keep the worlds in the dark. Almighty king, this is the opportunity to show your power from Death, that you alone can cast out the ETERNAL SPIRIT to Death so all worlds will be yours to rule as the Almighty King of Devils.

The kings in council began to clap. 'O' mighty king, you are the strongest devil in the world. This is the opportunity to put your strength to the test to fight this unknown spirit and it will be justified to rule all worlds forever with the power of Death.

The king of devils said; Truly I am the first king born of the seed of Death and all you kings gathered here is by my queen, its righteous I should fight this Spirit with all the power of Death implanted in me to rule all worlds for Death. Satan truly you are a prince you have become envious of my power and have become corrupt. You think you are better than me. My queen desire you, she think you are better than me. So I'll use this opportunity to tell you my prince and all kings gathered here in council, we are all brothers and live under covenant with Death.' You are a prince of all worlds and so shall you be. You can never be king of the worlds, let no devil king imagine he can be a mighty king like me, with the power of Death.'

Satan as I have said to you in the beginning. NO devil can change their nature.

Our Queen Mother always want something better in the world, it can't come by devils. Do you understand Satan? Spirits from the seed of Death can't change their spirit to be a Sprit in the light. This is the mystery spirit. Death held as his secret and it was revealed to me in a dream.

The king of devils said to the kings of their worlds; If we don't give Death the victory over the ETERNAL Spirit. Death want every devil an all from his seed to return to him.

THE LAST WARNING

The King of devils said; 'Satan, you were born to make devils to pass on the seed of Death. Satan, if you go against me you shall fall by the enemy of death and all from your seed shall fall to Death and never return in the worlds above.

THE QUEEN RETURNS TO DEATH

The King of devils found it strange his Queen had stopped crying for mercy.

The King said to the devils guarding his queen mother. Go and see if she escaped I don't hear her crying in the dungeon!' The guards went to unlock the dungeon, they went inside and saw the queen was asleep and light was in the dungeon. They then ran outside shouting 'HELP' to the king. The king replied 'What is the matter?' 'We went inside the dungeon and could not see, your queen has blinded us with light, a strange Spirit is inside the dungeon.

The king rushed inside and saw the dungeon was full of light and ran outside in fear, he called for his giant devils to go inside and bring out the queen. The giant devils ran outside of the dungeon screaming, blinded by the light. The king shouted 'My Queen, come outside! The news got out that the queen is blinding every devil that enters the dungeon. Devils came from all over.

The devils began to shout, O King, do not let the queen out, she is possessed by a spirit!' The King said to the queen 'come out'.

The queen came out of the dungeon, the King shouted 'you made contact with the Eternal Sprit she began to cry 'O King, have mercy on me. The devils began to shout, King cast the queen in Armageddon before this Sprit put a curse on all devils.

The devils began to shout, King, cast the Queen in Armageddon before we become accursed

The Queen began to sob, do not throw me into Armageddon, I'll never see you again O King, Death sent you and I together to make devils.

The King replied; I warned you to stop fucking with Satan, I am a jealous devil, soon Satan will join you to satisfy you with Death. When you see Death, tell him I sent you back to him because I could not satisfy you in the world.

The king told his giants to throw the Queen in the hole. The Queen began to make her way slowly to the lower region in Armageddon to Death.

She began to cry, O Eternal I am in Armageddon, my life is drawing nearer to Death, The devils has shut me inside this world to suffer punishment by Death.

O Eternal Spirit. I'm sitting in the lower region in this world, waiting for Death to punish me for returning to disturb his sleep.

Death woke up from his sleep and was in fear he when he saw the queen. He shouted where is your king? Why did you return without your king?

Death said; You are no more a Queen with out your king, you are back for punishment like the devils your King has sent me as an offering. When I fuck these naughty devils they cry.

Death said; 'Go and see if you can find a chamber, it's full up with naughty devils to satisfy you, the Eternal whispered in her ear 'Death is against me' she said 'O Eternal live forever.'

THE BATTLE FOR THE UNIVERSE

The Eternal in the light appeared before Death and said 'I command you to return to the chamber where you lock up devils sent to you to satisfy your lust in this conspiracy with your king to make devils with his mother to populate the worlds with devils to satisfy your lust.

King devil is like you, he want his queen mother punished by you in this world. You are despicable and all devils. The Eternal created the Spirit of fire and said 'if death or any devil come out of the chamber set Armageddon on fire!' Death began to cry 'peace, peace' The Eternal said to the Queen 'It is good you are here to witness the judgment I'm passing on Death for making devil to contaminate my worlds with disease.'

The Eternal said to the Queen; 'I am going to let you out to warn devils you made, what it will be like to suffer with Death for eternity. The Eternal said to the Queen; I'll set you free this time as I would not like you to be here when Armageddon becomes a world on fire'.

The Queen said 'Eternal, will I see you again?' The Eternal said 'Go quickly and warn all devils to depart from my worlds and go to the worlds beneath the earth. The Eternal returned to the lower region to Death on the chambers with his naughty devils. The Eternal said 'I've come in this world to execute judgement on you and all devils you hold in chambers of Armageddon. You have violated the peace covenant my making your Queen to make devils to populate the worlds to be against me. You have spoken to your King to be against me so I can't create Spirits by the WORD, because you have done this you will have no peace for eternity.'

The devils held in the chambers in Armageddon began to cry to Death save us from this severe sentence, let us out from the chambers.

Death said, my hour has come, I can't save you devils. The Eternal has spoken the word. He can't reverse, the WORD. His judgement is justified beginning with me and all devils. The Eternal created the Spirit of fire to set Armageddon on fire with Death. The naughty devils began to cry and tremble in front of the Spirit of fire. The Eternal said to the Spirit of fire, I've created you to judge Death and his devils in the worlds.

The final judgement will be between you and Elijah when CHRIST passed on the WORD to him for you to put the whole universe in the light as your victory over darkness. The Eternal said to the Spirit of fire; 'I am going to the highest world to take control of the universe when you hear the WORD, set the world of Armageddon on fire to put my worlds in the light from the earth to the highest world.

Day after day fire began to spew out all over Armageddon and sending up ash and rocks on fire to the worlds, the devils occupied, the devils began to run here and there in fear of returning to Death, loud explosion began coming out of Armageddon.

The queen appeared and said to the devils, to flee to the worlds beneath the earth. The Queen began to shout 'the worlds is about to be taken by the Eternal Spirit. The devils began to cry;' Oh king, a severe sentence has come upon devils. Boulders began flying out of Armageddon, smoke and ash followed by thunder in the worlds that has never been seen by devils, hot rocks, falling on the worlds, the devils vacated the worlds, there was much fear of Death.

Then there was silence in the worlds. The Eternal said to the spirit of fire set Armageddon on fire. Suddenly there was one big Explosion and Armageddon was a ball of fire, as it is today, known as the sun. The Eternal took his residence on the highest world he called heaven.

The earth was now the boundary between light and darkness, rotating around the world on fire with the first Spirit of the Eternal Spirit. To rule over darkness, after the final judgment by the WORD for peace and harmony.

THE FIRST JUDGEMENT BY THE WORD

After the judgment on Death in the fire in Armageddon (the sun) the Eternal began to create angels like himself in the light by the WORD with intelligence to have knowledge, wisdom and to be creative in all sciences.

The angels began to populate and built beautiful cities in their worlds and lived in excellent homes, living the perfect life, lacking nothing in their world. The Eternal created Ark Angels to serve him in Heaven.

The universe was now populated with angels in the light and devils in the worlds in the dark without Death. The earth was now the centre of the universe rotating around the sun with Death in fire. The Spirit of fire wait for Elijah with the Word for final judgement on godly sprits on earth to eliminate darkness for ever By the WORD.

THE KING OF DEVILS

The king of devils was furious that half of the universe was in light and occupied by Angels of the Eternal and began to blame his Queen and Satan and became cruel to devils who did not worship him anymore as the mighty king.

THE FIRST REVOLUTION

Satan gathered devils to start a revolution to conquer the worlds in the Light, his devils began going from one world in the dark to another an began to fight devils to take control of their worlds, when his devils got to the world with the king of devils with his Queen mother.

Satan said; The time has come to put your strength to the test, to see who will be King in the world! The King said because of you and my Queen, half of the worlds have returned to the Eternal, I warned you before, if you ever come against me, you will fall!

Satan replied; You will fall before me, I am no more your prince of the dark worlds, I am going to regain the worlds you have lost and I'll be the King to rule all worlds. The king and Satan began to fight, the other devils in his revolution joined in. Satan took a net and threw it over the king and held him down chained him and cast him in the dungeon and took control of the world with the queen of devils.

Satan told the devils in his revolution; I need strong devils to come with me in the worlds in the light to capture the Eternal and all his Angels he created. We have seen what the Eternal has done, which the Mighty King could not do with his power from Death. So let us prepare for this WAR.

Satan and his devil's took their sacks, put food and mouldy bread. The Queen gave Satan a cake to give to the Eternal as a peace offering. Satan and his devils left the worlds in the dark for the worlds in the Light.

When they got in the worlds in the light the devils saw big cities, beautiful Angels, lots of activity on building homes and construction of malls and botanic gardens. When the children saw the devils they started to stare at them, a little angel said where did you come from? Others called their mothers and fathers by mobile phone's saying hurry Father, there are strangers who don't look like angels.

Angels came from everywhere. An angel asked the devils where they came from. Satan said; we came from the worlds in the dark. Judge us not for the way we look, we did not come here to be sinners. We came to see how you dwell in the word in the light. There is much milk and honey and many cities built without walls.

An angel asked Satan who is your father? Satan said the son of Death. Another angel asked, did Death come with you? Satan said no he is in the fire in Armageddon.

Satan said; my father is a King, he is the first devil of Death, he is cruel and threatens to cast us in the fire to Death. This is the reason why we came in your world for asylum. An angel in the crowd said your garment is old and dirty.

Herod, an old devil said, 'Our king is not as creative as your Eternal we live in poverty, we are always hungry. There is not a lot of food to eat, we are run away devils, fleeing for our lives, our king threatened to return to us to Death. We're afraid of fire.

Satan said; 'we came from a long journey, we are tired and don't want to return. Our homes are burnt to ashes everywhere in our world is dust and big boulders from Armageddon. There is no water, we are constantly thirsty and have to travel far to fetch water.

Another devil said, balls of fire fell on my home, it was burnt to ashes, and our life is devastated and suffer because of Death. Satan said we came for asylum, to study. An angel in the crowd said to other angels, if devils live among angels, they will want to commit sin, we are warned by the ark angels if any angel fornicates with strangers, it's an immortal sin and its everlasting punishment.

Satan said; Death has done foolishly! We want to live in peace and not everlasting punishment with Death. We are not perfect like you angel, but we can live in peace if the Eternal accept us.

THE COVENANT OF PEACE AND STATUTES BY THE ETERNAL

The Eternal summoned Ark angel Michael and Gabriel to come to heaven He said 'Satan has brought devils in my world, the angels are curious and don't know where they came from, gather the devils together.

The eternal appeared in a flame of fire and declared a covenant of peace, statues and judgement on devils who seek asylum to live among angels on one condition, no devil is allowed to make a god with Angels or with my creation on earth or make an image of Death in my worlds. The Eternal said 'Satan you and your devils are in my world and asked for asylum to live and study in peace.

As long as devils live in my worlds among angels, they shall abide by the statutes of this covenant to live in peace and harmony and are free to return to your worlds in dark at any time.

After the Eternal spoke of his statutes and judgement, Satan and the devils prostate on their knee and said 'Eternal, you have spoken plainly to every devil, your statutes and judgement' We understand if any devil disobey and fornicates with angels or your creation on earth, is an immortal sin to provoke you and it will be justified to cast us out of your worlds to Death in the everlasting fire for ever.

The Eternal spirit granted asylum to Satan and 200 devils to live work and study and a free pass to return to their worlds in the dark. The eternal returned to his heaven, the highest of worlds and left Michael with the devils.

Ark angel Michael said to the devils, take heed of the statutes of the Eternal, let not your heart deceive you while you live among angels, lest every devil be cast out of the worlds in the light to end in the fire by the WORD.

Ark angel Michael said to Satan to warn every devil, they must live by the statutes for peace. It's not acceptable to pass on the seed of Death to make a god with the eternal creation by the WORD.

Before accommodation is granted, this document must be signed by every devil to verify they fully understand the judgement on devils if any go against the statutes of the Eternal Spirit.

Michael said 'Everything devils do will be recorded to make sure every devil live according to the covenant of peace and harmony whilst they live among the Eternal creation.

Satan Herod, Azazel, and every devil signed the covenant of peace. Satan worked in construction, Herod studied Astrology, Azazel worked in wine making, perfumery, others worked as labourers and tailoring studied engineering, electronics, satellite communications, space craft, music etc.

THE PROPHECY

The eternal summoned his ark angels in heaven and told them he's going to create his Christ to be a creator like him so he can take his rest from creation. The Eternal prophesied to the ark angels what CHRIST will do before he took office to create angels. Ark angel Gabriel wrote what the Eternal prophesied as a testament.

The ETERNAL prophesied, CHRIST will make angels in the light from his seed with Zion when they manifest their image shall be seen for seasons, years and days while they live upon the earth.

CHRIST will create Elijah by the word to manifest in the body of god after the spirit of god depart from the dead body for salvation, for Elijah to bring the body back to life to continue in the image to do Holy work to save Spirits of Christ and establish the Kingdom on earth.

Elijah will have the WORD from Christ to have power to judge devils and spirits of god's of the devils after they depart from kingdoms from the flesh of Christ and Zion.

Elijah will direct kingdom for salvation from Zion's flesh for CHRIST to create spirits to be among Angels in heaven.

Christ will put the whole universe in the light when Elijah speaks the word to Christ on the thrown to finish the work in creating Spirits in kingdoms for salvation.

After Christ put the king of devils in fire with Death, CHRIST will be in heaven to sit on the thrown to rule, when Zion sit with CHRIST on the throne she will see the final judgement on devils and godly spirits until the sprits of gods end in the kingdoms for salvation.

Elijah will be King of the world after he judge devils and godly spirits to fall to Death in the sun. For Christ to have the victory over Death and put the whole universe in the light with Angels in the light to live in peace and harmony without Death, devils, god's or darkness in the universe. After the Eternal prophesised what Christ will do? Ark angel Gabriel wrote the prophesy, put it in the ark in the new tabernacle as a testament.

THE PALACE

The ark angels built the most magnificent palace for when CHRIST and Zion took residence in Heaven.

THE NEW TABERNACLE

The ark angels built the biggest tabernacle for the angels from all worlds to come and congregate to worship the Eternal Spirit and praise him for all he has given them. Inside the tabernacle were two seats for when CHRIST came to sit and rule with Queen Zion. Next to the two seats, were two statues facing each other, an ark to put the testament, and a mercy sit.

The tabernacle was finished and fully furnished ready for its official opening. Angels began to make their journey with their siblings to see the new tabernacle for worship. Ark angel Michael began to give the good news that the Eternal is going to create his Christ to create angels to populate the universe so He can have his rest from creation.

THE CONGREGATION OF ANGELS

Angels came from worlds in the light to worship in the new Tabernacle. When all the angels took their seat inside the tabernacle, Ark angel Gabriel came forward with the prophecy of the Eternal and said to the angels, this is the Testament of the Eternal prophecy of all what CHRIST will do before he sit on the throne in heaven, he took the sealed testament and put it in the Ark, in the tabernacle.

The ark angels, Michael, Gabriel, Raphael and Uriel lifted up their hands to the eternal and all the angels in the tabernacle did the same and repeated after the Ark angels.

Holy Eternal Father, we give thee thanks for everlasting life and all you have given us by your WORD, CREATE your CHRIST.

The Eternal said Peace and love to all my creation gathered here in the tabernacle you have built to worship me. I'm going to create my CHRIST and Zion who will make angels like you and when Christ and Zion sit on the throne to create Sprits at the appointed time by the WORD

Celebrate the feast and give CHRIST praise when he is created to do all I prophesied he will do when he sit on the thrown to have dominion and rule all worlds with Zion with righteous judgment for peace and harmony in the universe for ever.

After the Eternal confirmed he is going to create his Christ to be a creator with the WORD. The Testament of the ETERNALs prophesy was placed in the ark to be opened when CHRIST sit on the thrown.

The Angels in the tabernacle began to sing Alleluia CHIRST, Alleluia Zion, come to our world, rule and have dominion according to the prophesy in the ark.

DEVILS IN HEAVEN

Satan said to the devils we have no hope to survive in heaven unless we capture Eternal and all of his angels. We are miserable and can't fuck angels to be happy, the Eternal is creating this CHRIST to spite us for our deceit and vanity to live among angels.

We do not know when the Eternal will create his CHRIST or what he will do to us, CHRIST will want to take over our worlds in the dark and we'll all end up in the fire with death.

A devil said; Satan, I heard from one of the ark angels the Eternal is going to create a man on earth and he will be lord among creatures and beasts with flesh. Another devil said Satan, I am miserable in heaven, let's go to earth and make gods with the creatures and they will pass on our seed and make spirits to populate the earth with multitudes of gods to fight with us to put the Eternal worlds in darkness.

Satan said; Every thing good in the world in the light is for angels of creation, unless we begin our revolution, we will be miserable living in suspense waiting to be kicked out of heaven if we made a god. Another devil said, Satan, I heard from the angels, where I work, if any devil made a god with the Eternal creation, when CHRIST is created he will create his Elijah, more powerful than the King of devils.

Another devil said Satan, I overheard from one of the angels where I work, Elijah is a god and he will judge every devil, and save Spirits with everlasting life. A devil said, Satan, if this CHRIST and Elijah send us back to our worlds, what can we do? We have everything here, except no sex with Angels.

Satan said ill tell you what we can do, let us declare war to take over the worlds of the Eternal before he creates his CHRIST to create his Elijah to judge devils.

I will take over his thrown and fuck angels to make gods in the heavens as our creation.

The throne is still without CHRIST. No one know when CHRIST will come or know what he look like or from what world he will come from to sit on the throne to rule the world.

THE SECRET OF THE ETERNAL

The eternal created the image of CHRIST in flesh and called the image Adam for CHRIST to sanctify and manifest with the WORD.

THE CREATION OF ADAM ON
THE ALTAR ON EARTH

Angels from many worlds came to earth to see the body the Eternal created in flesh called Adam. Ark angels, Michael, Gabriel, Raphael, Uriel and Joel ushered the angels to come forward to see Adam on the altar lying lifeless as though he was asleep.

One by one the angels bent on their knee and said, Eternal, you have created Adam in the flesh with splendour to have glory and they left the earth on their spaceships. Ark angel Michael; said, Satan tell the devils to come forward and worship Adam. Satan said I am not on earth to worship any creature in flesh it is Adam who should worship devils of Death.

We devils are in the world before Adam, and if he is rude to any devil when he wakes up from sleep, we will make a god upon earth to be his king before CHRIST is created in heaven.

The devils refused to worship they said Adam is flesh like the creatures on earth. Michael said; Satan If you or any devil touch the flesh of Adam CHRIST and his Elijah will remove all devils to a place where no devil has been before.

The Eternal spoke to the devils through the clouds above the earth; The image I call Adam is created on earth, by my WORD; Whatever WORD that come from the mouth of Adam will have wisdom, knowledge and understanding like me in the light, and will surpass every word that come from your mouth. The devils refused to worship Adam.

Satan said, Eternal let us put it to the test, if I fail to bring back the worlds to darkness, your CHRIST will succeed to put the worlds in the light with angles he creates, if not, Adam will worship the most barbarous god of devils.

The Eternal replied CHRIST will be aware of this challenge. ELIJAH will be the Judge. The Eternal went on to say I created all angels by my WORD I also created the Spirit of fire to satisfy your envy of me and my CHRIST for your arrogance. The devils left the earth and went back to heaven to plan for war.

THE MYSTERY OF CHRIST AND ZION REVEALED

After all angels and devils left the earth, Ark angels Michael, Gabriel, Raphael, Uriel and Joel gave praise to the Eternal for creating Adam. The ark angels stood in silence next to the altar with the lifeless body Adam.

THE CREATION OF CHRIST AND ZION

The Eternal spirit said CHRIST enter and sanctify in your image with everlasting life to make immortal spirits in the light as yourself in the flesh for their Spirits to be among angels in heaven after death of their body. The body Adam jumped.

The eternal said Zion enter the body Adam and cleave on to CHRIST with your Spirit with the holy egg and remain sanctified in his flesh until the appointed time to manifest. Adam woke up as if from a deep sleep and stood before the ark angels, they were the first to witness the creation of CHRIST and ZION in the body of ADAM stand and walk.

The ark angels served Christ/Adam angel's food and left CHRIST/Adam with Zion sanctified in the same body, Adam and kept the secret of the Eternal's creating his Christ different from angels in heaven. The flesh of CHRIST and Zion became the foundation to populate Immortal Sprits as CHRIST and Zion as themselves in the light on earth until the Spirit departs from their dead body to resurrect to the heavens to be among angels.

THE ETERNAL CREATES CHRIST IN THE BODY ADAM

The Eternal blessed CHRIST in his image while Zion was still sanctified and asleep and said to CHRIST 'When Zion manifests in flesh, she will have the holy egg to bare CHRSITS with your holy sperm which you will have at the appointed time. Tell Zion, when she manifest it is forbidden to make a god for the devils in your flesh. The Eternal took CHRIST/ Adam on a trip around the earth and spoke to him while Zion was asleep in sanctification.

The Eternal said 'CHRIST, in due time you will have sperm of light to make immortal spirits in the light like yourself and Zion.

A devil will come to earth with envy to tempt Zion to make a god to be in your flesh, you will have to wait until the salvation of the body of god to create your Elijah by the WORD to be the King in the kingdom and judge with the word.

When the time comes to create spirits in kingdoms for salvation it will be through Elijah when you are on the throne in heaven with Zion. After you create immortal spirits in kingdom the spirits you cast out,

Elijah will save the spirits that has faith in him to rest in everlasting peace.

To be ruler of the universe you have to have victory over the king of devils and cast all the devils in the dark worlds to death in the everlasting fire of the sun. After the Eternal told CHRIST what is to be done for righteous justice for peace and harmony in the universe.

The Eternal blessed CHRIST and Zion and went back to his Heaven to see what his Christ will to do according to his prophesy in the ark in the tabernacle.

CHRIST/Adam MANY DECADES LATER

CHRIST raised his hand to the Eternal and said 'Holy Eternal I am alone among creatures and all kinds of beasts, I am getting bore, Zion is still sanctified and I have no one to talk with on earth. The Eternal spirit answered 'I have heard your request my son, but have you thought how boring it is for me to be alone for eternity not having anyone to hold a conversation at my level. I have created you to have wisdom and knowledge and understanding to be a creator like me with the WORD to be the ruler of worlds. CHRIST/Adam answered 'Holy Eternal, you live on the highest world, I am still a Spirit, Manifest in Adam with Zion, Sanctified.

How can I populate the earth if Zion is not manifest in flesh to give her children that are perfect in your eyes? The creatures and beasts are populating and without Zion I can't populate like us in the flesh. The Eternal went on to say CHRIST, you have expressed yourself perfectly in your image without fear of me with good reasoning I know it wasn't good for you to be alone, but it was for you to be observant and judge what is pleasant in the world and to be creative with the WORD for eternity.

Zion shall now manifest in your flesh to be in her image to help you populate Spirits like yourselves on earth with the holy egg. but you will have to wait until the appointed time to have sperm to make immortal spirits.

The Eternal Spirit thundered and said 'CHRIST this was for you to know the difference between Adam and beast and creatures, they live and die, but you are a spirit like myself with everlasting life.

After Adams body is dead, you will separate from your image to do the work in creation through experience, not by me telling you but by knowing what you must do to be victorious over the king of devils and all devils in the worlds.

The Eternal said 'You have cultivated fruit of all kinds in Eve and have seen from one seed how it can grow into plants and how a pant can multiply fruit with seeds of its kind. CHRIST, it is not good for you to be alone, but it was for you to be observant and learn from creatures and plants and judge what is pleasant on earth and be creative with the WORD to make Zion share your joy for Eternity.

The Eternal said 'Zion shall now manifest to be in her image in your flesh to help you populate spirits like yourselves with the holy egg. You will have to wait until the appointed time to have sperm to make immortal spirits with everlasting life. CHRIST heard no more.

ZION MANIFEST IN HER IMAGE

CHRIST fell in a deep sleep after the Eternal spoke to him, Zion woke up from sanctification and said 'CHRIST, you can't populate without me, I want holy children like us in the flesh. CHRIST replied 'Manifest and you will be like me in your image in the flesh. Zion manifest in her image and cuddled next to CHRIST/ADAM waiting for CHRIST/Adam to wake up. When CHRIST woke up he saw Zion next to him, and she ran in the river.

CHRIST went after her. They embraced each other in the pool spiritually and bodily and began to kiss feeling their spirits, bonding in flesh with joy and happiness. It began to rain, showering blessings on them.

Zion cried I love you CHRIST, squeeze me tight, I want to feel like when we were together in Adam, to give my spirit strength and happiness. CHRIST said 'O beautiful woman, I will call your image Eve. She cuddled and kissed him, tears came from her eyes, happy to be free from the body of Adam. CHRIST/Adam picked up Zion/Eve in his arms and took her to his cottage to eat and celebrate to begin life together in their image in the flesh.

CHRIST/ Adam said 'Eternal Father 'Thank you for Zion I've called her Eve while she is in her image to keep the secret. The Eternal said 'Tell Eve to be observant and explain everything to her.

THE GARDEN OF EVE/EDEN

CHRIST/Adam showed Eve all there was to see in his botanical garden he called Eve before she manifest. Eve said 'WOW, did you cultivate all this for when I manifest? As they walked among the flowers they would let out their perfume scent, Eve held him and kissed him. CHRIST said 'everything you see I cultivated from plants from all over the earth that is why I call your image Eve, to share everything that is beautiful on the Earth with you when we are in paradise among angels. Eve said CHRIST, can I have past of the garden to help you with the work, I am a free Spirit like you and want to help you.

CHRIST said 'Choose any part you like but don't stray from my sight, I don't want the enemy of Death to come and snatch you away from me.' Eve said 'If this enemy came and snatch me from you, it will make me very unhappy to be separated from you, we are created to be together, let us not think about this enemy.'

CHRIST/Adam, said 'Eve the Eternal created me with the word to create and protect us, so it is important you are observant so you are not deceived while you are in your image. Eve said' If there is deception by our enemy, he shall live in fear of you with the WORD. If he assaults me, it will bring dishonour on him and from that day they began to work in the garden together then go to the pool after work.

CHRIST said; Eve, you are beautiful and the enemy will attempt to assault you to bring dishonour on both of us. If you are absent from me.

THE ANUAL FEAST IN THE TABERNACLE

Angels came with their siblings from all worlds in the light to the annual feast in the Tabernacle to give praise to the Eternal and to hear the news of his latest creation. Michael told the angels the Eternal has created his CHRIST with the WORD and he is coming to sit on the throne in heaven to do his Holy work in creation,

The angels began to sing and dance, 'Alleluia CHRIST Alleluia Elijah come into our world and join us' they began clapping lifting up their hands in the tabernacle saying 'O Holy Eternal Father, you created us by your WORD, we give thee thanks for everlasting life and your testament of your CHRIST to come and finish your work in creation by your WORD.

The Eternal said 'Peace and love to all my creation gathered in the tabernacle to worship me and give me praise for creating CHRIST to continue the work to create spirits with wisdom and knowledge to populate all my worlds with angels in the light from the throne in heaven by the WORD, then there was thunder after the Eternal spoke. The angel began to celebrate and dance and sing for CHRIST to come in the tabernacle to join them.

The devils did not go to celebrate in the feast for the coming of CHIRST, Satan said to the devils; I hate and despise these feast days. Another devil said to Satan, what can we do? We know nothing much about CHRIS, or what He will do to us. He might want to take our worlds in the dark and throw us in the fire with Death.

Another devil said 'I am miserable, in heaven we can't fuck with angels, let us go to earth and make a multitude of gods to make the Eternal and his CHRIST envy us. Satan said 'everything in the worlds in the light is for angles, unless we begin our revolution, we will be kicked out of heaven.

The devils debate in council

Satan and the chief of his devils began to debate among themselves about CHRIST and his Elijah that is more powerful than the king of devils in the dungeon.

A devil said 'I heard from the angels where I work that CHRIST will create his Elijah if any devil made a god with the ETERNAL, S creation to pass judgement on Devils and every god of devils. What do you think of this saying by the angel, Satan? What can you do? Satan replied i'll tell you what we will do, declare war and take over the worlds of the Eternal before CHRIST sits on the throne, and we will fuck Angels to make gods in the worlds of light.

A devil said 'Satan we will be fighting against the Eternal and his CHRIST and his back up Elijah. The angel said these three are called the Trinity, one looks after the other, and they are never in the same place together to catch them.

'Another devil said, I am afraid, if we fail this revolution what they will do to all devils, let us return to our worlds and you will be king with our queen. Satan said take hold of yourself I've got this plan to rule the whole universe before CHRIST rules from his throne. Another devil said Satan, I heard from one of the angels the Eternal has created a female in the flesh for Adam that is more beautiful than any angel.

Satan said 'All flesh is like grass, if I fuck her, she will make a god in her flesh to pass on my seed and all spirits from his seed will be my creation on earth, what is your problem? My brother, the only way is to go to earth and propagate godly spirits in flesh of creatures on earth.

A devil said 'Satan, I fear if I join you on earth I'll suffer for going against the covenant of the Eternal with statutes, its true I have strong desires to fuck angels, but its forbidden to devils to fornicate in his worlds. What more, it's an immortal sin to make a god to pass on the seed of Death. I'm prepared to suffer a little more for peace, suppose this plan fail, we can't come back to the worlds in the light to be among angels of creation.

Satan replied 'You fucking bastard, you are like those devils who doubt, you want peace and your penis wants to make war and capture angels in the light to make gods.

A devil said if we make a god, Elijah will remove all devils and return us to Death in the fire. Satan said. The ultimate plan is to declare war to bring all the worlds to darkness, to be the king of the universe.

Satan asked Herod; can you detect from which world CHRIST will come from your observatory, Herod replied I can not tell all I know he is on his way. We are forbidden to have sex with angels I suffer this celibacy like you Satan, I can't say yes for peace or no for this revolution to fight against the Eternal's creation.

Satan replied; You are a devil like us and if any devil made a god with the Eternal creation, it will brake the covenant for good, so think about this, there is much temptation and have to suffer celibacy or return to Death if I made a god with angels.

THE OATH

Satan said 'We have debated in this council and everyone has signed the oath in this meeting to declared war against the Eternal and CHRIST and Elijah to take over the worlds in the light as out ultimate desire according to this Oath. Satan told the chiefs of devils in council to pass on the declaration of war to the devils by word of mouth in secret while he visits the queen of devils.

THE VISIT TO QUEEN OF DEVILS

Satan got an exit pass to visit the Queen of devils and journeyed to the ancient worlds in the dark, when she saw Satan, she said I know you would be back to give me a devil that looks like you. Your king is still chained in the dungeon, I told him, you will come to take his place as king of devils.

Now you will be my king Satan, our king has become old and weak, come and make me happy in this miserable place. Satan replied, My queen mother, you had knowledge of Death, I am like you, I want to do good but I'm wicked like Death' There is a CHRIST and his Elijah coming, I fear what they will do to devils with the WORD. My queen, no one knows who they are, and angels say CHRIST is coming and what more, the Eternal has created a man in flesh on earth, now this man has a woman that is driving me crazy to fuck her and make a god. It will be our new creation.'

The Queen opened her legs wide and said Satan, you wanted me to give you a devil to look like you, come and fuck me and put your seed in me to make a devil with all your malice, hate hostility, jealousy and sexual desire and rage and envy to make war instead of a god in flesh of this woman, I suggest you leave this woman alone, she is a temptation to destroy devils.

If this woman make a god, Elijah will remove you and every devil an gods from her flesh, when CHRIST come to remove sprits of gods in her flesh.

Satan said I will give you this devil if you make sorcery for me to see our future, the queen said Satan, I can see this beautiful woman, she will take my place in the world to produce like them on earth. Satan said; my queen, what can you see again for the future, The Queen replied I can see you will be a king with another beautiful woman and she will have a god for the god of the first woman. He will take over to control gods on earth from your throne on earth and you will come back to me to live in a miserable place.

Satan said, my queen, what do you see again for the future of devils? The queen said, If you leave me and go to the worlds in the light you will return to me, if you go to earth to make a god with this woman, you will leave much confusion and trouble to gods on earth, after all devils to return to Death.

The woman will say the godly spirits in her flesh, belong to devils she is a creation of the Eternal on earth. Satan, it will be the end of devils in the worlds in the dark to be in the everlasting fire with Death. According to the covenant, I and king devil had with Death, he wants every spirit from his seed to return to him if we fail to populate all worlds with peace and harmony.

Satan said, My Queen mother, see if there is any hope for devils to succeed over this CHRIST and his Elijah, the queen used her sorcery and said I can see multitudes of godly spirits falling in fire crying and you will wish you fucked me instead of this woman on earth.

The queen said; Satan, if you leave me to go to earth to make a god with this woman, I'll be a goddess and she will be queen. Satan, leave this woman, she is a temptation for disturbing the peace in the universe and we will all end in the everlasting fire with Death. Satan said goodbye to the Queen. She said' you will be back to me.'

THE SECRET THE DEVILS DID NOT KNWO

The secret Satan and other devils did not know, CHRIST is the spirit of Adam and Zion is the spirit of Eve, both spirits created in their image in flesh, CHRIST was created by the WORD to create Elijah to have the WORD to remove all devils and godly spirits from the earth by the WORD.

Satan's journey to the earth

When Satan saw Adam and Eve naked working in their garden together, he hid in the bushes, envying Adam with jealousy and hate and wanted to kill him to take Eve away. but was in fear of CHRIST, who he did not know. From the bush he looked at the naked body of Eve with lust to rape her, waiting for a chance for her to be alone. Adam and Eve put their garden tools in the shed and stopped working for the day, and walked towards the pool in the river naked. Stopping now and then on the way, to kiss and hug each other.

A lion came from the thicket and began walking towards Adam and Eve, it stood on its hind legs and put its forelegs on the chest of Adam, Eve began to stroke the hair of the lion. Eve went on the back of the lion to the pool for a swim, then lion left the pool and walked away, to be with the lioness and cubs.

Satan became more jealous seeing Adam and Eve splashing water on each other and diving in the pool and coming up together to breathe air, laughing and embracing and kissing.

Satan climbed a tree to have a better view to peep at Adam and Eve, the monkeys on the trees began to squeal when they saw Satan, guinea fowls began to fly, making a lot of noise to draw Adam's attention.

Adam and Eve came out of the river, walking hand in hand toward their cottage, to eat and rest for the evening. While Adam and Eve was asleep, Satan was in the bush, when the wolves saw him they began to howl, frogs began to croak an creatures in the night began to screech to wake up Adam, but Adam was in a deep sleep.

Satan became hateful to man, beasts and creatures on earth and wanted to go inside the cottage to kill Adam but because of the fear of what CHRIST would do, he stayed in the bush for the night.

SATAN RAPED EVE TO MAKE A GOD

Adam was asleep, Eve got up and went to the garden, Satan came out of the bushes, he called Eve, Eve, looked. Satan came towards her, excited. Satan said I am the prince from the other world and I was sent here to teach you and Adam what is good and what is bad in this world, so no evil can come to you on earth.

The queen of my world has sent her greetings and wishes you good luck. Eve in bewilderment said you are supposed to be celebrating the feast in the tabernacle in heaven, why are you on Earth? Satan said I was sent here to teach you and Adam landscaping while angels are celebration, and to protect you and Adam on earth from the enemy of the Eternal.

While talking, Satan pulled Eve towards him, Eve said, do not touch me, I do not like you touching me. Satan said; you are a beautiful creature, I want you to be my woman. Eve said. There are beautiful angels in heaven, you have to go back, or I will call Adam to remove you from the garden. Satan became furious, Eve did not like him to touch her and threatened to call Adam, he held her and wanted to kiss her, she cried go away from me.

Satan hit her, and threw her on the ground, pulled her under the apple tree and raped her with vengeance and hate, Eve screamed, help, Satan hit her and she passed out. All the leaves on the fruit tree fell and covered Eve, in desperation and fear of the consequences for raping Eve, Satan made his way back to heaven and began boasting to the devils what he had done to Eve, to make a god in her flesh.

ADAM AND EVE

Adam woke up from sleep and went into the garden to join Eve, he saw the leaves on the trees had fallen covering Eve, she was fast asleep. Adam said; Eve, wake up. She woke up from sleep trembling. What have you done? You are trembling, Eve replied. The prince of the other worlds raped me, he took my virginity.

Adam said, the devil seed is in your womb, it will make a god in your flesh. in tears, you shall bring this god to live until salvation to create Elijah to be your Son in creation by the WORD. Eve the bastard has left heaven to come to earth to rape you, to bring shame on us

The Eternal Spirit whispered in CHRIST/Adam's ear; 'In the time of salvation, you will establish the kingdom of god, create Elijah by the

WORD and pass on the WORD to Elijah to do the work with you in Salvation.

After god is born, you shall have sperm to make Spirits in the Light with Zion holy eggs to be among angels in heaven, you have the WORD to protect you and Zion, until you create Elijah to do the work with you in the time of salvation.'

VENGENCE IS MINE CHRIST SAID TO ZION/Eve.

CHRIST said to Eve; 'Vengeance is mine, woe to every spirit of gods I find in your flesh after I remove them they will return to devils if they have no faith in Elijah to save them from devils.

Zion/Eve said its better, I stayed sanctified, I've brought much trouble to you as I'm manifest in my image let me sacrifice this body, so I can be Zion and you will be free. I feel unclean with this god in the same body I'm in. what can I do?

CHRIST/Adam said 'there is not much you can do, after you give birth to this god it will live until salvation comes to create Elijah to save you from any attack by devils in the future.

CHRIST/Adam said 'Eve, go to the pool in the river and wash yourself and pray to the Eternal to have mercy for being pregnant with a god from a devil.

SATAN RETURNS TO THE HEAVENS

Satan told the devils in his revolution; the mortal sin has been committed, I've fucked Eve to make a god and there is abundance of creatures on earth with flesh. The time has come to declare war and challenge the Eternal for the worlds in the light and capture all his angels in heaven.

SHOOTING STAR WARNING

The Eternal sent a shooting star to CHRIST to be aware of the devils coming to earth to use the WORD to defend himself and Zion.

Satan and his devils stole spaceships to fight against the Eternal and his angels and began blasting at the telecommunication in heavens and destroying spaceships to have control. The Eternal summoned his Ark Angel Michael, Gabriel, Joel, Raphael and Uriel and said; 'Satan has gone to earth, he raped Eve to make a god, the devils have now broken the covenant of peace, now they have declared war on me to take over my worlds in the light. Gather a legion of angels from the other worlds and chase every devil back to their worlds in darkness.

The angels came with well equipped spaceships with the latest technology and joined Michael and they began to attack Satan and his devils. When the devils saw spaceships coming towards them, they made a run for the worlds in the darkness as they got to the boundary between light and darkness, Michael and the legion of angels began shooting lasers at the spaceship, the devils stole and destroyed all. The devils fell to their worlds in darkness.

THE DEVILS ARE CAST OUT OF HEAVEN

The Queen said; Satan I told you, the woman on earth is a temptation for devils to fall, you have failed with your revolution, Satan said, my Queen, I am returning to earth to make gods for our worlds. The Queen said; Satan, you will bring us to ruin, there is enough worlds for devils to populate devils. Why do you insist to make godly spirits in the flesh of creatures? This CHRIST and Elijah will return spirits of gods to Death, because they are of the seed of Death.

The Queen said; According to the covenant, Death says he wants every devil from his seed to return to him if they disturb the peace and harmony in the universe. If spirits of gods come here, they will have no flesh, there is little water and much drought in our worlds the godly spirits will cry to you, to save them from Death in the fire.

Satan said; If we take over the earth, you will be queen. The gods will be your subjects to fight for the earth with us. The queen said; Satan, all devils who follow you to earth will be captured and will end in the chambers awaiting judgement for rape.

Satan said to the devils; cast out of heaven, I want every one of you that is fit to fight CHRIST and Elijah for the earth for Death, to make the testament of the Eternal in the ark obsolete for the universe to be in darkness. We must capture CHRIST and Elijah before they bring the whole universe in the light by the WORD.

Satan said to the giant devils Emin, Magog, Golieth, Annak and Zuzamzim; 'I want you to come with me to make giant gods to fight for the earth. Satan handpicked 200 of the strongest devils to come with him to populate the earth with gods and promised them that they will be kings on earth.'

The Queen said; Satan, there is little water and much drought in our worlds if godly spirits come here they will cry to you to save them from thirst'

SATAN RETURNS TO EARTH WITH 200 DEVILS

Satan returned to earth with 200 devils an he went in search of Eve, he saw her standing in the pool in the river with a stone on her head, he came to the edge of the water, shedding tears and said; Eve come out of the water, I have some good news for you. The Eternal sent me to intercede on your behalf, so come out of the water. Eve replied; go away, I don't want to see you, or be seen with you, I hate you for taking my virginity, you are deceitful, you rape me and now I am pregnant with a god from your accursed seed.

Satan said; O, Eve, it is because of you and this god in your belly, I left the good life in heaven to be with you, so come out of the water to be with me. Eve cried; go away, Satan got angry, said, either you come out of the water willingly or I come and get you out forcefully to take you away with me. Which way do you want it?

Eve cried, go away from me, you rapist and trespasser in my flesh to make a god in sin. Satan got angry, took a deep breathe and blew on the water and the water parted left and right, an Eve stood in the river naked.

Satan got excited, seeing Eve naked, he tried to pull her out, Eve screamed; Adam, Adam, help me, the devil is trying to rape me again. Adam heard her cries and began to run as fast as he could to the river, He saw Satan pulling Eve out of the river, CHRIST/Adam said; go away devil.

Satan fell on the ground by the WORD and backed off. Satan shouted insults; O, Adam, all my hostility, envy and hate is for you, having a good life in the midst of Ark Angels and now I am among creatures like you and your woman on earth'

Adam said; Satan, your presence is hostile towards us, you frighten the creatures on earth, why don't you go back where you came from? What is our fault? You say we are creatures, yet you come to earth and rape Eve and she is pregnant with your god in her womb, we are created holy pure in the flesh by Eternal, your god is a trespasser, an will be born in holy flesh in sin, we have caused you no harm or injury, why have you returned to earth to pursue my woman? You will go to hell for raping Eve.

When Satan heard he will go to hell for rape he became afraid he would end with Death in the fire, Satan said to Adam; you being a creature, what do you know about hell? Tell me! The Eternal created you in the flesh to live among wild beast and creatures.

I am in the world before you it is I who should have your beautiful woman as you are inferior to me, when I saw Eve I said to myself ill make a god to look like me on earth, to be my creation and he will be a King, now I am expelled from heaven because I raped your woman.

Adam took a fierce look at Satan and said; Warn other devils on earth, if they trespass in holy flesh, CHRIST will come with Elijah, and remove you and them from the earth an send them to a place they have not been, or heard off so leave in peace an don't return.

Satan went on his horse, confused and afraid, if he came after Adam and Eve again, CHRIST and Elijah will come to remove all devils from the earth.

NINE MONTHS LATER

Eve said; Adam, I'm in pain, she began to cry O Adam, help me, Adam began to wipe the sweat off her face. While giving birth to god, pushing, Eve said; Adam, this god is afraid to come out I am suffering birth pains for the god of Satan, its no joy to bring a god on earth to suffer like I am suffering. The birth pain increased, Eve began to cry louder and louder in pain O, O, O, god, come out from me, she began to tremble, her heart racing in fear an uncertainty about this god.

Adam said; Eve, I will put eternity between you and this god in your flesh until its spirit leave the earth, cursed are all spirits who pass on his seed to make gods like him in your flesh. If this god is a rapist like Satan, he will leave the earth to suffer like you are suffering with this birth.

Eve said; Adam, the god won't come out, It's afraid to come out because you are next to me, so, go take a walk, maybe his kind come when you are not around. Eve went by the wild cane reed by the river and did as the creatures give birth, she opened her legs over a pile of grass and god came out and began to yell.

Adam heard the yelling and came quickly picked up god and washed off the blood. Eve said; what name shall we call him? Adam replied; let us call him Cain Eve breast fed god in the name of Cain.

AFTER THE BIRTH OF god (CAIN)
Jn8.43-47;1Tim3.5-7

After the birth of god, CHRIST/Adam had sperm of light, so no devil could say god is a son of CHRIST/Adam. After Zion/Eve had a Son for CHRIST/Adam they called him Abel and a daughter they called her Tamah, they looked different from god of Satan.

End of the first episode.

EPISODES
2 *and* 3

THE BIRTH OF CAIN (god)

After a couple of years, CHRIST (Adam) said; 'Holy Eternal father, this god (Cain) looks peculiar like devils on earth, he is not like me or Zion (Eve), Eternal, if I do not have sperm, this god will be heir of my house, I want a Son to be heir of my house.'

The Eternal said; 'CHRIST my Son, if this is your desire, you shall have sperm to have a blessed Son with Zion (Eve), to make many spirits, the same as you in the flesh until their spirits to resurrect to be with angels I've created with everlasting life.'

THE BIRTH OF ABEL (Jesus)

Zion (Eve) gave birth to a son for CHRIST (Adam) and they called him (Abel) Sprit name Jesus then Zion (Eve) gave birth to a daughter for CHRIST (Adam) and they called their daughter (Tamah). Sprit name Jerusalem The five lived together.

SATAN AND god (Cain)

CHRIST (Adam) brought up god (Cain) the good way, CHRIST (Adam) said; 'Cain, if you obey me, you will live long on earth and rest in peace, of late you have no respect for me, your mother, or Jesus (Abel). Cain said; 'Jesus (Abel) told me you are not my father'.

Cain spent a lot of the time grazing his goats in the field, one day, he saw Satan in the bush looking at him and his heard of goats, Cain said 'What are you doing here?' Satan said 'I came to see you, to ask CHRIST (Adam) for you to come and spend some time with me.'

Satan asked CHRIST (Adam) 'Can Cain come and spend some time with me, so I can get to know him, Adam said; 'If he desires to be with you, he is free to go and learn about devils.

IN THE PALACE OF SATAN

Satan said 'Cain, you are my first god on earth and you live under the covenant between devil and Death. Therefore, you must fuck Tamah to make a female god, to make gods for us in her flesh, so you can be heir of the earth. After indoctrinating god (Cain) with conspiracy.

Satan and some devils, eager to see the beautiful Zion (Eve) returned with Cain. Satan said 'There is no other god like Cain, except he has Tamah to give him many gods from her flesh.

Adam said; 'Satan, as long as god (Cain) do well and obey, he is accepted, but if you want him to have Tamah to pass on you accursed seed, this is no acceptable! Abel said to Satan; 'You have no respect to ask my father for Cain to have to have my sister.'

Adam said; 'Satan, you and your devils leave my yard and do not return! Satan, this is the second time you came before my face, next time CHRIST will remove you and all devils from the face of the earth!

Satan and the devils became afraid of what CHRIST will do to them if they stayed and rode off on their horses. Adam said to Cain 'it is in your nature to do what Satan tell you to do. I don't want you to see Satan any more.'

THE CONSPIRACY

Satan came lurking in the bushes in the garden, peeping at Tamah (Jerusalem) naked, watering plants, god (Cain) saw him and said; 'What are you doing here, if Lord Adam see you, he will be angry with me. Satan said; 'god (Cain), either you fuck Tamah to make a female god for you, or I'll take her away to make gods for me. So slay Abel and she will me yours to make gods for me. I f you don't do as I say, I'll kill you and you will end with Death! So make up your mind, I am your father, not CHRIST (Adam) so do as I say. Ask Abel to graze his sheep with your goats, slay him and you will have Tamah.

In fear of Satan, god (Cain) said 'Abel, I found a new pasture, come and graze your sheep with me' When they got to pasture 'Cain took a sharp stone and hit Abel on his heard, Abel fell on the ground, crying in pain, loosing a lot of blood. Cain fled from the scene.

CHRSIT/Adam said 'Zion (Eve) I can hear Abel crying, lets go and look for him. Adam met god (Cain) running away, he stopped him and asked him where is Abel, god/Cain said 'I don't know' CHRIST (Adam) said what have you done to my Son!?' 'I heard him crying for help' god (Cain said I'm not a herder of sheep, neither am I his watchman.'

Adam said 'I heard Abel's (Jesus) Spirit crying out to me, where did you put His body? You cursed the earth, now you shall go inside the gate of Hades for shedding holy blood on earth.

Cain replied 'My punishment is greater than i anticipated, if Satan find me, he shall slay me, if I'm out of your sight!' Adam replied 'The day Satan slay you, your kingdom shall be for salvation for killing Abel in the conspiracy'

Zion (Eve) said 'god (Cain), all you have given me is sorrow and pain from the day I gave birth to you, don't come back, you killed Abel (Jesus) he was a good Son!

THE RESURRECTION OF JESUS (SPIRIT IN ABEL)

CHRSIT (Adam), Zion (Eve) and Tamah (Jerusalem) gathered wood and put the body Abel on the pile of wood, they sang songs to say goodbye. CHRIST (Adam) asked the Eternal to send and Ark Angel to show Jesus the way to be among Angels with everlasting life.

CHRIST (Adam) set the pile of wood on fire to burn the body Able, suddenly there was one big flame of fire and in the fire, Jesus appeared and began to walk on air going towards the cloud, waving goodbye to CHRIST/Zion and Jerusalem and went into he cloud to be with the Ark angel.

CHRIST/Adam said the WORD for the wind to come unto the cloud to take Jesus and the Ark Angel to meet the Eternal Spirit in the heaven of heavens.

AFTER THE RESURRECTION OF JESUS

CHRIST/Adam said; Zion/Eve, I love you, god (Cain) doesn't know the secret, we are Spirits in our image, we brought up god (Cain) the good way but since he began to mix with devils, he became bold, he always wants to be with them. Cain's spirit is not accepted in heaven.

Zion/Eve said; 'my lord, Cain has too many faults, you allowed him to do what he want, he hate me and always reminds me of rape, he blamed me for being born, saying it was because of me, the devils was cast out of heaven.

CHRIST/Adam replied 'There is not much I can do but to direct him to do good for his spirit to rest in peace after his spirit departs from your flesh for salvation to begin in the righteous way by the WORD. I told god (Cain) if he did good, he could live long on earth, as long as he doesn't fornicate with Tamah (Jerusalem) to make a god like him, from the accursed seed of his father, god (Cain) said to me I am inferior to his father, I told him if he disobeyed, Elijah will be righteous in the flesh of his mother, he said I was stupid and the devils were superior to me, and he was the prince of the earth.'

CHRIST (Adam) said; 'I told god (Cain), Abel is of my seed, he is my heir, god (Cain) said he is the heir of the earth, Abel (Jesus) had told him to shut up and have respect for his Mother and Father. 'Jesus/Abel told Cain he is the heir of my house and not him and he got angry.

CHRIST (Adam) said; 'Zion (Eve) darling, we are in this uncomfortable situation in our life, regardless of disappointment, I accept god (Cain) is not perfect like us but when salvation come, you will be satisfied with Elijah in your flesh to be the judge and saviour with the WORD.'

MUCH SORROW

Jerusalem (Tamah) asked her mother what Elijah is like, Zion (Eve) replied; 'My daughter, Elijah will save you from devils on earth, have faith in him so you can be his Queen and he be your King.' Jerusalem (Tamah) said; 'Mother, so you and I will be Queens in the world?' Zion/Eve said; 'After you've over come much temptation my daughter'.

CHRIST/Adam said 'My daughter, when Elijah is created, he will be my first Son in creation, he will give you children on earth and they will be among Angels in heaven with us, when he begin his work in salvation in kingdom from you flesh through me.'

Salvation

Tamah asked Adam/ CHRIST to explain what salvation is. 'CHRIST/ Adam said 'Well, my daughter, the devils are on earth and want flesh to make gods to pass on the seed of Death to make godly spirits as their creation in our flesh. When salvation begin, Elijah will direct kingdoms for salvation to come and remove spirits of gods of the devils and create immortal spirits like us to continue in their image until the spirits depart from your flesh and resurrect to the heavens like Jesus and you will be satisfied with children that are good in your eyes and accepted by the Eternal Father in Heaven. Elijah will keep an eye on your my daughter, he is your saviour and King.'

The devils plan to capture Zion (Eve) or Jerusalem (Tamah)

A young devil said; 'Satan, let us hide in the garden and pounce on Zion (Eve) or Tamah and take off with rapid speed, god (Cain) is of no help to us.' Another devil said; 'Satan, CHRIST (Adam) can't stay in one place with his woman and daughter all the time, let us split in two division, wait until Tamah stray from CHRIST (Adam) and Zion (Eve) and capture her to make gods for you and us.

Another devil said; 'Let us keep surveillance on the hut of god (Cain), if Tamah visits him, we will Kidnap her.' Another devil said 'If we capture either, where are we going to put our capture?

Satan called; 'Azazel, Show him the plan of the dungeon, where Eve or Tamah will be kept In captivity to make gods. The devils agreed to rotate watch on Adam, and the hut of god (Cain) to take one of the women when they visit him.

CAKES

Zion (Eve) said 'My Lord, I had a vision and saw your power in the future with the WORD before it happens. My lord give me this Elijah to destroy the bastard who raped me to make his god (Cain), he hates me and has no respect for you.

CHRIST/Adam visited god (Cain)to see how he was getting on, when Cain saw Adam he pretended to be sick and said; 'My lord, I miss Tamah and long to et some of her cakes, when CHRIST (Adam) was about to leave, to return to Zion (Eve) and Tamah, god (Cain) said; 'My Lord, next time you visit, bring some cakes for me.

Satan and the devils visited god (Cain). Satan went inside the hut, god (Cain) said 'the Lord left a little while before you came and we be bringing me some cakes on his next visit.'

CHRIST (Adam) Zion (Eve) and Jerusalem (Tamah) were celebrating a feast, Tamah (Jerusalem) made cakes and there was mush left over, after they had eaten. CHRIST (Adam) said; 'I'll take some cakes to god (Cain) tomorrow.'

The next day, CHRIST/Adam had to plough and plant corn and told Tamah (Jerusalem) to take the cakes to god (Cain) 'It will cheer him up, Zion (Eve) said; 'Lord, I don't want Tamah (Jerusalem) to visit god (Cain) I would take it myself but I want to finish this ploughing before the end of this day.

Tamah took a basket with the cakes to give to god (Cain). Zion (Eve) said 'Be careful, and come back straight away' When Jerusalem (Tamah) got to the hut, she said 'I brought you these cakes', god (Cain) took the basket of cakes and began eating them hungrily. He reflected on what Satan said 'Fuck your sister and pass on my seed, so she can have a daughter to make gods.'

CAIN DISOBEY ADAM

Cain said; 'Jerusalem (Tamah), 'Why haven't you visited me?' 'You stay in the Lord's house. Jerusalem (Tamah) felt sorry for him and went to sit next to him, god (Cain) held her and began to kiss her and fondle with her. Jerusalem (Tamah) pushed him away and said 'Stop what you are doing to me!'. Mother will hate you more if you do anything to me, god (Cain held her down and said 'You are going to give me a god to be like me' then he raped her. She conceived his godly seed, to make the son of god (Cain) Tamah (Jerusalem) left the hut crying and returning to CHRIST (Adam0 and Zion (Eve).

Satan and the devils who were spying on the hut rushed and grabbed Tamah. Satan went inside the hut and strangled god (Cain) until his body was dead!

Satan held Jerusalem (Tamah). She cried, 'Let me go!' Satan said; 'In hell, I'll let you go.' From now on, you will be my hell.' He put Jerusalem (Tamah) on his horse he called Death and all the devils began to ride their horses with great speed to the mountains to get away.

The godly spirit of god (Cain) came out of his body and was carried away by the wind an fell in the mouth of Hades in fire to await judgement for rape.

CHRIST (Adam) ZION (Eve)

Zion (Eve) said; 'My Lord, Tamah (Jerusalem) should be back by now, let's go and fetch her from god (Cain). When they went inside the hut, god (Cain) lay on the floor dead with a broken neck.

SALVATION

Zion (Eve) began to cry with hysterics, O Lord have mercy on me for bringing up this god to distroy us. CHRIST/Adam said 'Let us take his body out from this filthy place and wash him clean for salvation.

THE TRINITY—THE ETERNAL WITH THE WORD, CHRIST WITH THE WORD, ELIJAH WITH THE WORD

CHRIST (Adam) presented the body of Cain for salvation. CHRIST (Adam) said, my Eternal Father, I present to you the dead body of god(Cain) from the flesh of Zion for salvation to create Elijah by the WORD, It is righteous for me to bring back the body of god for Salvation to create the Spirit Elijah by the WORD to serve me in the kingdom of god. We tried to go forward but god (Cane) disobeyed and followed the devils, he did the opposite to destroy us. O Holy Father, let the Spirit Elijah sanctify in the body of god full of grace to be my Son and helper in creation with the WORD.'

Suddenly, the cloud began to cover the earth, the Eternal spoke in the cloud 'My Son, create your Elijah, it's according to my prophesy written as a testament in the Ark, what you will do if the devils made a god to create your Elijah by the WORD to be your Son in creation with the WORD to serve you kingdoms of gods from your flesh and Zion (Eve) at the appointed time to create Spirits in kingdoms for salvation by the WORD.

Your request to create Elijah is granted to remove the devils from the Earth and godly spirits when you return to create Sprits to establish the kingdom on earth world without end.

ELIJAH IS SANCTIFIED IN THE KINGDOM OF GOD AND BRINGS THE BODY

The sun with drew its light and the whole earth was in darkness, Zion (Eve) said 'Lord, speak the WORD so Elijah can come and sanctify in the body of god to continue in his image to be like us in in creation. Christ said Elijah come and enter the body of god to be my helper on earth.

The body of god (Cain) stood up and Elijah was in the image of god, full of grace and honour in the kingdom in the flesh of Zion (Eve) to do holy work on earth, as the saviour and judge over all on earth.

Eve fainted and fell on the earth in fright, CHRIST (Adam) looked at Elijah in the image of god, Elijah looked at CHRIST (Adam) and said 'You called for me to take over the kingdom of god 'I am here to serve you in the kingdom and help you to have the victory over devls of Death.

CHRIST (Adam) embraced Elijah to serve Him and save his Peoples SPIRITS and serve him kingdoms for salvation to created Spirits in the Light. The trinity with the WORD. Zion (Eve) woke up and said 'my Son created in my flesh, now I am satisfied, Elijah you are my saviour on earth.

Elijah said 'After I cast out the devils from the earth, your flesh shall be your inheritance for CHRIST to create Spirits in the Light for ever.

THE GODLY SPIRIT OF CAIN CRIES IN HADES

The godly spirit of Cain began to cry 'O Lord it is better my mother's womb was my grave instead of being born short of glory to suffer. Curse all gods born from the seed of devils to end as a godly spirit like me without flesh of my mother in this heat in the earth.'

'Curse Satan for raping my Mother to conceive me in her womb, O Lord, remove all devils on earth they want to destroy you and my mother with gods on earth. O lord I am in this heat, dying of thirst.

Let all devils who think they are superior to you, hear my cry day and night for conspiring with them to take Tamah in captivity.' Satan encourage me to rape Tamah to pass on his seed to make gods to inherit the earth.

Oh Lord, I had no faith and was disobedient and trusted the devils, I am ashamed for raping Tamah, to make a god to be like me, now I am suffering for a moment of joy.

CHRIST (Adam) REPLIED

'Though you were no help to me when you lived in my flesh, your body was not yours. All flesh is mine. You lived in it with disgrace, from the seed of Death.'

'You have passed on the accursed seed of devils from Death in Tamah to multiply your unholly seed in my flesh.

I warned you to stop lusting for Tamah and if you had faith in me, you could dwell and live to an old age, and have exemption to rest in peace on earth and not suffer in fire for rape.

'Since you left your kingdom vacant, it was righteous for me to create Elijah to sanctify his Spirit, to bring back your body for salvation to life to continue as my Son in your image, now my spirit is satified with Elijah in your mothers flesh. My first son in creation, you chose to follow devils, that was your choice.

'Every time Elijah, lift up your right and left hand, to me in the time of salvation is for me to come and cast out spirits of gods that has passed on seeds of devils in Tamah's flesh will be your inheritance in the fire for raping Tamah.

'I've put everything in the hand or Elijah, he will make what was impossible with you, possible on earth for everlasting peace and everlasting life. So be patient in the fire until Elijah release you to warn all spirits of gods in my flesh to have faith in Elijah to rest in peace.

DEATH IN THE EVERLASTING FIRE

CHRIST (Adam) prepared his white stallion Faithful, and Elijah took the red stallion, they began to look for tracks and saw a lot of hoof marks from horses and began to ride south in pursuit of the devils for days. Satan looked back and could see two horses coming at them far off

The devils split in two direction, some went with Azazel others went with Satan towards a cave in the mountain, Satan helped Tamah down from his horse and put her inside the cave and rolled a stone at the entrance an joined the other devils and went out of sight.

CHRIST and Elijah looked for Tamah for seven days. Then Elijah said My lord go back to the compound to be with Eve, mean while Ill persue the devils on my own and will bring Tamah back to you

Elijah began to search on his own and on the the third day, he saw a high wall that was was built between the mountains and in the middle was a gate as high as the wall. Elijah spoke the WORD and the gate fell, inside was a palace satan built with the devils. When the devils saw Elijah they became afaid and called satan.

Elijah went inside the palace and began to search for Tamah, and saw a big altar, Elijah looked under the altar and saw a certificate god/Cain had signed in the conspiracy to kidnap Tamah, saying he was Tamah's husband and he sold her to Satan.

Elijah said what is this contract of marriage you have with the Lord's daughter with Cain? what has my Lord done to you? you have killed your god, so you can have his sister by his mother.

You have taken the Lord's daughter unaware of this conspiracy to hold her captive. Tamah left her Father and mother's house without knowing of your plans or having knowledge of this plan.

Elijah said; Satan you have done foolishly. In so doing you took Tamah captive after Cain raped her to make a god like him. You murdered your god/Cain to take his sister for yourself. Where is Tamah?Satan it is in my power to harm you, take heed you do nothing bad to the Lord's daughter.

Satan said; we are devils cast out of heaven and we came to earth, we are strangers on earth. If my god raped raped Tamah to make a god like him, I have I have an inheritance from my god for passing on my seed in her womb and the sprit that is born from her flesh is mine, the flesh of the sprit that is born you can present to CHRIST, He delight eth in the flesh of Adam and Eve.

You be the Judge. I have not fucked Tamah. What is my tresspass? what is my sin? it is Cain who raped her to make a god like him. You have persued after us and searched all over my palace before the other devils and found not the Lords's daughter.

Elijah said; CHRIST will watch between you and I. After I leave leave you and the other devils. Elijah commanded a pile of stones to fall in the palace ground from the sky and said, every seed that is passed in Tamah's womb to make godly sprits will fall like the pile of stones on top of each other to you and Death.

One of the devils said; Its because of Eve we are cast out of heaven, and we are living among creatures. Now you come and accuse us of murder, conspiracy and rape, you should be glad the poor bastard is suffering for his sin in fire like Death.

Another devil said; You persue us like a thief caught in the act to punish us before our time end on earth. If Tamah concive Cain's seed, remember Satan passed on his seed in her mother's womb to make a god in her flesh flesh and if Tamah concive a god for Cain we will accept as one of us.

Elijah said; make sure father and his god dont go with the daughter of Adam and Eve in my absent to make godly sprits in her flesh, to face the final judgment like you on earth and Elijah departed.

THE OATH

The devils put back the gate that fell after Elijah left and shut it, waited untill Elijah was out of sight and went to the cave rolled the stone from the entrance and put Tamah on the horse in the name of Death and the horse took off with Tamah on its back. The devils began to chase after Death with Tamah on its back.

Tamah tried to get away and came unto rapid water flowing downwards to awaterfall, both horse and rider was in the air and landed in a deep pool at the bottom of the mountain. Tamah held on to a branch because the current of the river was fierce going downwards.

The devils came down the mountain looking for Tamah and held her captive again. She cried, let me go! the devils tied her up so she would not escape and brought her to the palace and put her in a dungeon.

The devils debated what they should do, fearing trouble if they touch her. After the meeting they brought Tamah out and said what have you to say?

In fear, Tamah took courage and said unto the devils, I know you were cast out of heaven and came to earth, and Death has fallen in fire. My Mother fainted after one of you raped Her to make god/Cain in her flesh.

My mother told me she was in the river praying to the Eternal to have mercy on god in her womb and a devil came and blew on the water while she was in the river naked she began trembleing before the devil who raped her in the garden.

Therefore I pray you swear unto me by my Father and Mother and my Lord Elijah and other brothers and sisters I may have on earth

Satan answered, let us make an oath for life. I will deal with kindly while I am on earth, if I and the other devils are not on earth you will be blameless of the spirits of gods from the seed Death in your flesh.

If you go out of this palace gate and make a god for god/Cain, Death shall claim his godly sprit. All godly sprits from his seed belong to Death, so you will be guiltless of sin with me when I an the other devils are no more earth if you agree to this oath.

Tamah answered, according to your words, so be it, till I am free from this oath if you are no more on earth, an the other devils an their godly spirits from my flesh on earth and she was held in bondage to this oath to be FREE till devils are no more on earth

THE BIRTH OF THE son of god (Cain)

Satan built a smal temple in the palace, Tamah would go in the temple an cry while she was pregnant for god/Cain to come and save his god from Satan who threaten to kill the baby god if i was a male.

She would cry, o god I am now a mother of your god in my womb and satan is blaming me for making a god for you, he said, its because of you he is on earth among creatures like me an will eat your god from birth if its like you.

ELijah appeard in the temple and Tamah said, Cain/god surely you can help me, she didn't know the devil had killed god (Cain) when she was held captive, and Elijah was created by CHRIST/Adam with the WORD an was in the image sanctified. Tamah thought she was speaking to Cain.

Tamah said, let it not displease thee. I cannot return to my Father an our mother to bring your god in my Father's house after what you did to me. I am ashamed, I am now pregnant for you and am held captive by Satan, I cant bring your god to my Father and Mother to destroy my family like you.

Tell my Father, Ill take the blame for bringing cakes to you, Ill pray to Elijah who is to come in this world to take care of me and my affliction and sorrow for the birth of your god in the palace of Satan.

I think you go now before Satan find you here, he hate you. When the Elijah will give me children from my flesh for SALVATION.

LABOUR DAY

The day came to give birth; Tamah was in much pain, Satan sat with a bowl of salt waiting for the birth to eat if its a son for god (Cain). Tamah began to cry, O Elijah save this god

Satan gave her a slap on her face and said bring this fucking god for me to eat, Im hungry for his flesh. You fucking bitch bring him on to teach your mother fucker she should not give birth to a god to rape you to make a god in my palace.

Its because of her god Im on earth, leaving the good life above to end with a crying bitch on earth in bondage, Tamah began to tremble, her legs shaking, an in fear and holding on to the birth not knowing if its a male or female god.

Satan began to shout, bring this god forth or I will pull it out with my hand. Tamah began to cry its not my fault! Its not my fault this fucking god is not ready to come out on this earth to be eaten by you, its afraid of you.

Satan said; Go to the temple and pray to your mother and ask her what you have to do. Tamah slipped out of the palace and went to a place where she had prepared to give birth in the bush. She opened her legs and the baby god droped on the grass in the bush.

Tamah cried, O Elijah save this baby god, and she returned to the palace. Satan said angrily what took you so long; a small black cat was curling around his legs, Satan threw it against the wall and killed the cat. Tamah picked up the dead cat and went outside, dug a hole and put it in an covered it with earth.

Elijah herd the son of god (Cain) crying in the bush, still in his mothers blood with its navel uncut and took the baby god away cleaned him from the blood from his birth and clothed him in badgers skin and fed him with milk from goats and honey from the rock.

Tamah returned inside the palace. Satan said, now come and make this god. Tamah said when I went to bury the cat, I gave birth to a baby god. Satan rushed outside the palace and returned and said, Tamah, what did you do to this god of my god I saw blood on the earth? Tamah said a lion eat it instead of you.

Satan went outside, put his finger in the blood on the earth and began to lick his finger and began to feel lust to fuck Tamah. He rushed inside and held her with hate for denying him the pleasure to eat the son of god from birth. Tamah began to cry, dont dont kill me have pity on me.

Satan pulled her toward him, Tamah cried no, no, dont rape me. Satan said Im going to hell for you she began to cry, help, help, Satan raped her and she passed out. Satan called the two eunuchs and told them to take Tamah to the dungeon, feed her and prepare her for an offering next full moon.

THE FULLMOON OFFERING

The devils had a council meeting for the preparation for the feast offering to initiate their rite to make gods with Tamah according to the oath.

Bazalel, when he was in heaven was trained in all manner of skill, he came to the dungeon to take Tamah's measurement, he gave the eunuchs oil he specially forulated to massage and stimulate her body to prepare for innitiation and gave them instruction to teach her devils language and give her food to put on weight.

Some devils made an altar outside for the sin offering for gods to pass on their seed to ppulate the earth, and others made an altar inside the sanctury to initiate Tamah to make gods according to to the oath with Tamah.

Inside the sanctuary devils were trained to keep the fires burnng and to assist on the brazen altar.

THE DAY OF THE FULLMOON

The devils brought gifts to Satan and gave him praise for bringing them on earth and sang songs, O Satan sit on the throne and be king to rule over devils on earth, they put a crown on his head and sang o godly sprit in the heat save the king.

Satan had a vision and saw the godly sprit (Cain) crying and warning Him if you touch of the Lord's you will be held in captivity in flames like me for rape and every godly sprit from the seed of devils will return to you and Death without Tamah's flesh.

After crowning Satan as king, the devils gathered around the altar in the sanctury. The devils outside killed a bullock and brought its blood inside the sanctuary and sprinkled its blood around the altar. Took the fat and cast in the fire, took the head of the bull and staked it on the altar in the sanctuary.

The trumpeter blew his horn. King Satan came an sat, the devils sang song of praise to be the first to fuck Tamah to be the mother of gods. Twelve of the high ranking devils came from outside dressed in the skins of beasts, crocodiles, mask of hawks, and the mark of the serpent on there head.

The high priest took incense of musk, cinamon, calamus, casica, coco oil, jasmin oil, palm oil and threw it on the fire in the sanctuary, the santuary was filled with fragrant smell. Then their was silence with great anxiety to initiate Tamah under oath.

The two eunuchs brought Tamah from the dungeon and they lay her on her stomach on the altar she was afraid to look at the devils. the devils outside the palace began to dance at the beat of the drums.

The twelve high rank priests cast lots, who would be the first six to initiate Tamah, and they to the right of the altar and the other six went to the left. the first six sprinkled blood of the bull over Tamah and began to lick the blood off her back. The other six took blood of the ram and sprinkled over Tamah and began to lick the blood off the back of Tamah while satan was playing with himself.

HORN OF THE BULL ON THE ALTAR

The eunuch gave Tamah a cup with liquid to drink and it began to stimulate her, then told her to kneel and hold the horn of the bull on the altar to take the oath to be a goddess to make gods.

King Satan took his time, scared, hearing the crying of the godly sprit (Cain) in the heat warning him if you rape the Lord's daughter you will join me in the fire in Hades to wait for the final judgment.

The high priest brought Satan a cup with the bulls blood and he became horny and it stood up like a cucumber and he went on the altar and raped Tamah. Tamah fainted, she concieved seed and the eunuchs took Tamah to the dungeon.

The devils outside killed a sheep, took the breast and brought it to Satan to eat raw with its blood. Satan got lust again and commanded the eunchs to take Tamah to his chamber. They oiled her up and gave her liquid to drink and brought her to Satan. She began to cry Jesus, Jesus come and save me from this devil.

Satan held her down and said you want JESUS? Ill give you JESUS and began to f . . . . k her wickedly with all his malice and hate for holy people. And she passed out. Satan called the eunuchs to take her back to the dungeon. No other was allowed to fuck her.

THE HIGH PRIEST PROPOSE TAMAH
TO BE THEIR QUEEN

King Satan sat on his throne and made Herod the high priest for devils. Herod said O king! Tamah is pregant with your god to make gods to live by your law of devils under the covenant of Death. Tell Tamah we will save her Mother and Father from Death if she accept to be your Queen on earth

The eunuchs brought Tamah to the High Priest; he said your life is more valuable than us, fear us not but Death, so make alot of gods for us and we will save your Father and Mother from Death.

Every god you make will worship you as their mother, you must do what our king say to populate the earth with godly sprits to give your Father and Mother double from your flesh for Salvation.

What Christ will do with so much flesh on earth we do not know, it is a hidden secret, we looked in the mystery book, but it was in fine print in heaven in a language we dont understand.

So when gods begin to pass on the seed of devils to make sprits in your flesh, the more flesh their will be on earth it will make your Father and MOTHER happy. Our king is highly inteligent and the power of his seed will populate the earth with his malice and hate for all all angels in heaven

Tamah said! O king it will be justified to give you back all the godly sprits from your seed and what Christ do with my flesh of my Mother for salvation will be justified for holding me in bondage. Tamah asked; o king what will CHRIST do to godly sprits in my flesh, now you have made me pregnant with your god?

Satan said : I dont know what CHRIST and ELIJAH will do as it is writen in fine print, but an angel said the two can put all devils to flight, so gods will have to fight for the earth for Death. The Eternal much mystery attached to CHRIST and Elijah which no devil have seen.

Satan continued to say no devil know who they are, or where they will come from that is why we keep you in captivity because we live in fear of what the two will do to us for being on earth among the ETERNALS creatures.

TAMAH BE COME QUEEN OF THE EARTH

The high priest said; satan the devils want Tamah to be your queen Satan said; Tamah kneel before me and worship me before the devils, Tamah said! I only worship my Father. Satan said kneel before me, he took the crown from Herod the high priest and put it on her head and said you shall no more be called Tamah but queen Tamuze.

ELIJAH ADOPT THE SON OF god

Elijah brought up the son of god fed him and called him Ammon, he grew up and called Elijah Aba. Elijah taught Ammon all manner of skill and craft to be a ruler among gods, Ammon was good with his bow and arrow, a good herder of ox, sheep and goats,

Elijah told Ammon he would make him great among the gods of the earth if he had faith in Him, his sprit would rest in peace for ever and a New Sprit would be created to sanctify in his body to be his SON of Elijah in creation.

Ammon asked; What is sanctfied? Elijah said I am sanctified an glory in the body of god your father. I am in his image. Ammon asked; show me your glory. Elijah said; If I show you my glory, you will die and your sprit will see my glory, but one day when you are old and die you will see my glory.

You are a sprit from the seed of god your father in the kingdom and all sprits from your seed shall enter the gate of my enemies after they depart from the kingdoms if they dont have faith in Me. The blessing shall be in kingdoms of gods for salvation to create new Sprits to continue on earth untill their body die to go to heaven.

Elijah gave Ammon knowledge of Him in the kingdom of god, and told him the kingdom of gods is for Salvation and he must obey and have Faith in Him as long as he live on earth for his sprit to rest in peace. But if you deal falsely with me and tell lies you will have no everlasting peace after your sprit depart from your kingdom, your sprit is not like me in the image of god your father.

Elijah said; Ammon I brought you up to rule gods and show them the right way, and to teach gods to have faith in me to rest in peace before they die

Ammon began having dreams and said; Dady im drawn to this mountain, what is up their? Elijah said; Your Mother is held in captivity up there, you should go and save her from devils. Ammon said; Dad surpose she dont want me to save her what shall I do?

Elijah said; Tell her Elijah of her Father brought you up and she must depart with you. The WORD which I speak through the mouth of god you father is with me from her Father.

Ammon meditated on what Elijah said, it did'nt make sense, who is Elijah in the kingdom of god his father, he knew no one else but his dad, now He is talking about Elijah is talking through the mouth of god with the WORD of his mother's Father.

Ammon had a problem understanding Salvation and creation of Elijah by the Word and with the WORD in the Kingdom of god (cain) of the devil. Ammon began to be rude and arrogant and agumentative an felt he didn, t need (Elijah) Dad anymore and must move on with his heard to experience life on his own.

Elijah said; Ammon it is righteous for you to go and save your mother from the devils. I am always available to save her. I promised her

Father to save her. When she call for my help I will do so, at the moment She has not asked for my help.

Elijah went on to say; Ammon before we part from each other, I forbid that you should tell anyone Im your father as long as you live. If ever you become spitful, rude, and be arrogant to your mother I will abandon you.

You shall not fornicate with your mother, or do as god your father did to make you with her. If you fornicate with her you will pass on the seed of god your father to make gods for devils, but you can fornicate with gods like yourself born from the flesh of your mother.

When the time for Salvation your mother will inherit kingdoms from her flesh from sprits from your seed, which is not holy accepted in heaven, godly sprits from your seed will return to you an Death if they have no faith like you.

The time came; Ammon rounded up his herd, mounted his horse, took his bow and arrows took all his herd and Elijah and Ammon sepparated an went their way.

Elijah visited CHRIST (Adam) and ZION (Eve)! They had many children, and their Sons and Daughters had many children, Elijah took his rest until CHRIST separate from Adam to begin his holy work with CHRIST by the WORD

SEED TIME

CHRIST (Adam) and Zion (EVE) had many Sons and Daughters awesome SPRITS like themselves in the flesh and populated there part on earth, there was much order an disipline, they built a tabernacle where they would gather and learn Scripture, there was much to eat and drink, well cultivated pasture, no sickness, no death and lived a great distance from the devils in peace.

Satan, made ten of the devils kings and gave each of his godly princesses to the kings to be their godly queens to populate their nation with gods to make godly sprits to live unto Death.

AMMON son of god (Cain)

Ammon was now on his own with his large heard of cattle, goats and sheep going from place to place making his way to the mountain. One of the pirinces in the palace saw Ammon with his heard coming up the mountain went to Satan, and said! O king of devils their is a stranger coming toward the palace with a large heard of all kind.

THE FEAR OF CHRIST AND ELIJAH

Satan said; Go and keep an eye on him, he told the devils to take Queen Tamuze in the dungeon quickly thinking its Elijah coming.

He and the devils went to spy in the bushes to see who it was when they saw it was a god that looked like the gods in the palace, the devils threw a net over Ammon on his horse and brought him down and took him inside the palace and lock him up in chains, and took all his herd.

Satan called the other kings to have a meeting to discuss the fate of Ammon., when the kings saw ammon, he looked looked at them wild and fierce. One king said; Satan, certainly he is a god, but not from my nation, other kings said he is not a god from their nation. A king ask Ammon where he came from? Got no reply. Another king said CHRIST and Elijah must have sent him to spy on us, another king said if Christ and Elijah is against us, why should they send us this god with a large herd of cattle and goats, another king said; Satan, did you kill god of Eve? Satan said, I am suere he was dead after I strangled him in his hut.

Herod the high priest of devils said; Satan why dont we bring out this mysterious god before us and ask him where he came from and who sent him, and why he is among us and our gods.

THE CENTURION

The centurion on watch brought Ammon before the Kings. Satan asked, who are you; Ammon did not understand their language, Satan called for the devil that study the behavior of creatures an began sign language, Ammon looked outside and saw a lioness feeding her cubs, and put his finger in his mouth and began to suck pointed at himself.

The kings began to laugh. Satan said, you are a babylion and shook his head, Ammon began to laugh. Satan began to scratch his head, wondering if he could be the god he wanted to eat from birth that disappeard, standing in fron of him.

Satan said to the kings, he is a god ill adopt him. Satan called his servants and told them to taech him to speak like us and bring him next fullmoon to converse with me, feed him and cloth him like one of my princes and brand this forehead with the mark of a serpent

NEW MOON

Ammon was brought in to meet Satan in his chamber to converse, and he explained he came from a far country and was brought up among creatures and wild beasts and he was happy to be living in the palace. Satan called for the high priest and told him to teach Babylion the covenant of devils with Death.

Within a few months, Ammon could converse and learnt to live by the covernant of devils with Death. an taught the princes of Satan how to live among creatures, the princes began to hate him for being more inteligent than them.

Satan and queen Tamuse invited the kings of devils and there godly queens to a banqet and he boasted about Babylion was more inteligent than his princes and some devils, an asked the high priest to bring Babylion to introduce him to the kings, when he came he stood before Satan and the kings, Satan said when you first saw my adopted god he could not speak, now he can speak and he is a teacher to my gods, I will no more call him Babylion but Judah.

One of the kings said; if he is has to have this name he must accept the covenant of devils and Death, an all sprits from his seed to live unto to Death an if he should seek CHRIST and ELIJah he should die like the creatures on earth

Satan called Judah and said! Judah you must swear by the covenant of devils with Death to live unto Death as long as you live on earth.

Judah knelt before Satan and queen Tamuze and said; I swear to worship king Satan and queen Tamuze to live according to the covenant between devils and Death. Satan said now you shal be one of my princes in the palace.

The trumpeter blew his horn an announce to all devils and gods Judah is a Prince in the palace of Satan. Judah rejoiced he is now a prince an can go in and out of the palace as he pleased. Satan gave Judah a chariot, so he and the princes could go huntig wild beast and shoot birds with bow and arrows and chase godly women.

Judah became popular among the gods, he built palaces for kings in their nation and pyramids to sacrifice gods for their spirits to be with Death he trained gods to shoot bow and arrows for war. The devils began to like Judah as their favorite god.

The devils were populating gods, and gods began to passing on their seed with godly women making gods and populating their nations much faster than the people of Adam and Eve's people.

MANY DECADES LATER

The devils asked Satan we have populated gods on earth but CHRIST and Elijah has not come to earth to attack us, Satan said may be they have no interest in the creatures of the Eternal on earth so we can now go and capture the people of Adan and Eve.

THE BATTLE FOR THE EARTH

The devils did not know Christ was the Spirit of Adam with the Word and He had Created Elijah by the WORD in the dead body of god/ Cain to serve Him Kingdoms for Salvation when he is on the throne in heaven. Save the Spirits of his people and resurrect them to him in heaven after he has the victory over the king of devils in the ancient worlds in the dark.

THE THRONE IN HEAVEN IS FOR CHRIST

While CHRIST is sanctified he has no spritual power, He has passed on the WORD to ELIJAH in order to take the other half of the universe he has to chalenge King devil of Death and cast all devils in the ancient world to Death in the fire to establish the universe in the light with angels with everlasting life according to the prophecy of the ETERNAL and testament in the ark in the tabernacle what CHRIST will do before he sit on throne in heaven by the WORD with His Elijah, before he create Sprits on the throne in heaven.

To establish the kingdoms on earth with Spirits in the Light from sprits of gods that has faith in Him. To dispense True Justice and righteous judgment for CHRIST to rule in all worlds in the universe populated with angels in the light with everlasting Life to live in peace and harmony according to the new Testament by the WORD.

PREPARATION FOR death

All the people of CHRIST (Adam) and ZION (Eve) gathered together in the tabernacle to hear CHRIST; CHRIST said, my children the devils are planing to make war on us, when they come use restraint.

I am a living SPRIT in this body and every one of you from my seed shall live forever, but in order to have Eternal life, I must sacrifice my body, so I can be a SPRIT without flesh to resurrect to the worlds in the light.

Christ went on to say my children, you are living SPRITS in the light living in your image in the flesh of your Mother and Myself, no god has a sprit like yours in the kingdom, the gods live unto Death after they die they will be godly sprits of the devils.

In the time of salvation the kingdoms of gods will be created to have new Sprits in the light to continue in their image and the godly sprits that has faith in Elijah he will save from Death. Elijah do not interfare in human affairs, as he is the judge of the whole earth, but will abide till you sabbath to resurrect you to be with me where no god or devil will make war on you my people.

Christ went on to say; My children I cant be a ruler of the worlds in the light while I am a Sprit in ths body, (adam) Elijah is created to save you, and have power over all devils and gods and to Pass righteous judgment on all devils and godly sprits, and will only save godlysprits that has faith in him to rest in peace on earth.

The devils and gods cant see you are Sprits in the light even to this day and think we are creatures that live and die like creatures in the flesh. CHRIST (Adam) said to the congregation in the tabernacle; We live in peace, but the devils are planing to eliminate all of us from the earth. When the BATTLE for the earth begin you will be SPRITS in heaven and will see the victory over devils and gods an paradise regained by the WORD.

The people in the tabernacle cried, O lord let us fight the devils an remove them from the earth with their gods before they eliminate your people Lord

Christ said; My children the devils will be driven from the earth by righteous Justice and righteous judgment when the hour come, for all to be removed at the same time for commiting sin, at the moment only Satan has commited rape and made a god in the flesh of your Mother an hold your Sister in bondage in captivity to make gods in her flesh. My people it is expedient I separate from this body so I can be a SPRIT to do the work Im created to do. Every ONE of you are Holy SPRITS same as Me and your Mother and Elijah will save you when you are Sprits to be with Me.

Elijah is mighty in all secrets of righteousness, He is your Saviour, and him only you must trust after I leave to do holy work I am created to do, Elijah is the Judge of the whole earth and the weightier work is in His hands until salvation end in your mothers flesh. All the people said Amen

Christ said; My children I have given you knowledge of the new testament in the ark before I am separated from this body (Adam) I have enjoyed being with you on earth. Have faith in Elijah to save you. All the people said Amen.

My children I am harassed and have grief of what will happen to you after I depart, the devils are training their gods to make war on us while you lived in my presence with your Mother you did not fornicate with gods of the devils, or taken anything belonging to devils. When your hour come to sepparate from your body you shall be holy Sprits ascending to heaven to be among angels.

My daughters Christ said; the devils and their gods will find every opertunity to lead you astray to concieve their seed to make godly sprits in your flesh to do the same like devils now on earth. The Eternal was angry when the devil raped your mother and she concieved god (cain) and he did the same and raped your sister before he was killed by the devil, now they are planing to eliminate us from the earth to take the kingdom by force.

My children my hour is coming to offer My body for oblation to do the work im created to do for peace and harmony in the world, *I know you will* have distress after I am away from you. Eve cried O Lord, let Me share this offering with you, we are created together, let me share this pain with you, she began to cry this is more than I can bear ill be consumed with grief without you, this is much to bear, O Lord. CHRIST (Adam) said have faith, Elijah will save you.

Eve went wondering and crying, knowing what the devils will do to her people, suddenly Satan appeared on his horse. Eve shouted, you accursed devil if you touch me Elijah will come to remove every devil and gods from the earth,

This put fear in Satan he rode off in haste in Fear. Eve went back to the tabernacle and told her people what She said to Satan. They gave praise to CHRIST and Elijah an began to sing and felt confident in their Savior Elijah.

THE DEVILS PREPARE TO TAKE
THE KINGDOM BY FORCE

The devils were angry of the warning by Eve if they eliminated her people CHRIST and Elijah would removing them and their gods from the earth and suspended the attack on the people of Adam and Eve and continued to teach their gods to fight.

Judah taught his battalion how to shoot by bow and arrows and to fight with cutlasses and spear for war, he taught gods agriculture the way Elijah taught him and raise cattle and other livestock, their was abundance in the nations.

The devils taught gods music, tailoring put gods in governments to rule in nations under the kings, they taught gods whichcraft to heal the sick from godly sprits, do sorcery and grow food by the fullmoon to bring abundance of food in their nation and to bring the first born female gods to their king for harems.

THE BANQUET

Satan invited the kings and the commandants of gods of their battalions to celebrate his success and wealth in the nations with queen Tamuze, mother of gods. Every king brought his godly queen and princesses and princes other devils brought their godly women.

When they were gathered together, Satan gave a speach and boasted, from the strength of my seed in my queen's flesh, I have given you Kings the best of my princesses to populate gods in your nation and through my master builder Judah there is much prosperity.

So let us give Prince Judah praise for teaching our gods and setting up my government, and commerce among the gods, he has become a prophet to the gods to live by the covenant of devils with Death.

Satan thanked the Kings and other devils for teaching gods the arts, to paint, make carve images of their kings to worship them when they are absent, and to do sorcery, magic for gods for their kings, and prepareing the gods to take over the earth by force

Satan went on to say! My vision is to bring the Universe back to darkness and to be the king of all worlds. All the devils began to clap, hail cezare, after his speach. The cooks served smoke ells, smoke rats and other smoke creatures as a delicacy to start, some devils had thirst for blood with a little salt on there black puding before the main course was served.

The gods began to play music for the kings, and belly dancers came to put on a show for Satan and the kings while eating, after dinner, the gods began to play music for dancing with singers singing to the beat of the music never before herd by devils.

SATAN TEMPT JUDAH

Satan said to Judah the princes tell me you are a good dancer among the godly women, dance with Queen Tamuze let me see the both of you dance. Judah took Tamuze to the floor to dance, and she became excited an began to wigle her buttock to the music of the gods.

Satan said what is this dance? Is his to make me jelous? Satan had kept Tamuze from seeing any one, and had her face covered so only he could see her face. Judah was angry he had to return her to Satan. Judah knew she was his mother and kept this to himself.

THE COUNCIL MEETING

The ten kings of the nations sat in council to discuss the elimination of adam and his people from the earth. One king said, Satan we are enjoying life with our queen from your seed and populating our nation with gods. If we go an eliminate Adam and his people from the earth, Eve warned you CHRIST and Elijah will come to remove us and our gods from the earth. It will be the end of gods in her flesh.

Another king said, Satan, after the banquet with you and Tamuze, I had a chance to think of your vision so far we have much success in populating the earth with gods form the seed of Death, let us postpone this war on Adam and Eve and their people.

We have much flesh now from our godly women to populate gods to make godly sprits, we have much choice now, and in time our gods will fornicate with the women of Adam and will pass on our seed to make godly sprits in their flesh. Adam an his people has not populated the earth as fast as us an our gods.

Satan replied; I know what you are saying and have thaught about it myself, but I am angry and have much hate, contempt and malice to kill Eve because the god I gave her is now fucking our goddess, the mother of devils with Death. Im with this creature and she cries and call me a sinner and rapist, she is not happy and always ask me to be free she is not like your godly queens like she devils.

If we have to survive on earth, we have to eliminate Adam and Eve and all their holy people from the earth so we can conquer the earth with our godly sprits to distroy all flesh in the world, we are kings on earth and will make Judah the prophet an commander of all godly sprits after we distroy all flesh so there will not be holy people of the Eternal on earth to make us be in Fear of CHRIST and ELIJAH.

Though up to this day I dont know where Judah came from, I made him a prophet to our gods and has authority over our gods to lead them when they are godly sprits. At the moment he is a god, and has taught gods agreculture to grow food for our gods to eat in the nations.

Another King said Satan I am proud of your fearless prince, he is good at every thing, you had him to blaspheme Christ and Elijah and to hate them all his life to death of his body. Adam and Eve are like Thorns in your eyes. Some gods have reported when they go and steal fruit in the holy nation, the holy people walk about naked and they are tempted to rape their women.

Satan, this excites me, as it excited you when you saw Eve naked, and want to go and steal fruit to see these beautiful holy women naked, but I fear if we Kill Adam and eliminate his people there will be no hope to achive your vision to be king of the world.

Satan replied; I am a great king with the hardness of heart to do more evil than king devil from Death I chained, for loosing half of the universe to the ETERNAL with the WORD. When we were in heaven we saw beautifull angels and according to the statuets by The ETERNAL no devil was allowed to fuck Angels, we are cast out of heaven and we have a problem we cant fuck holy women of adam and Eve., now our gods are tempted to do the same as me to commit rape with lust for flesh like devils. It is devils who gods will blame for making gods to lust in the flesh of Adam and EVE.

THE WAY OUT

Satan said; We have to eliminate Adam and his Sons from the earth to stop his seed from populating holy peaple, and take the holy women captive so we can bargain with CHRIST and Elijah to leave us alone or we kill all the women if they attack us on earth.

Another king said; Satan, there is another way to remove this fear of CHRIST and Elijah; Let Judah take a battalion of gods he has trained go and kill Adam. CHRIST and Elijah cant have reason to remove us from the earth because its gods that will kill Adam and not us.

The fear of CHRIST and Elijah is not in Judah, he and every god in his battalion has made an oath to execute malice, hate, kill, rape, steal, decieve, and mislead others in their life time on earth. Satan you have made Judah prophet to our gods to live by the covernant with Death. So let Judah execute death on Adam for us, and his battalion of gods will be our witness to say its Judah who killed Adam an not devils.

IN ZION I CREATED THE JUDGE

All the kings agreed, that Judah should go and kill Adam; The high Priest invited Judah to join the kings. So far Judah has kept the knowledge of Elijah in the kingdom his secret and want to make aname for himself to be a ruler.

Judah was brought in to join the the kings. Satan said; Judah you are a master in every thing you do, there is famine in the nations and our gods are geting agitated with hunger, disease, and fighting each other for food. Their is much food in the nation of Adam and his people.

Take the battalion of soldiers you have trained and go and kill Adam, leave the rest of the holy people for us kings to deal with, when you kill Adam report to me in the palace. This is your first mission to prove to us kings you hate CHRIST and Elijah, we expect success from your hand.

Judah left the meeting with the kings in haste, put on his coat with many colours and told his battalion of soldiers to arm themselves with bow and arrows and prepare their horses to ride with him on a long journey to the holy nation of Adam. The battalion left in the night fot the long ride to the holy nanion.

USE RESTRAINT

CHRIST (Adam) gathered and Eve gathered all their people in the tabernacle. Christ (Adam) knew His time had come to put his plan into action. Christ kissed Eve, and everyone in the tabernacle came foreward to kiss him and gave them a hug.

Then He said; My children, my time has come to do the work I am created to do, while my Sprit is in this body I cant do nothing, neither can Elijah do his work on earth in righteousness. The hour is at hand for Elijah to execute righteous justice and judgment on all devils on earth.

CHRIST. (Adam) said my children give no god a reason to attack you. Use restraint. I am living you on earth in Peace. Judah is coming in our nation with his battalion of soldiers. I know you will weep after I am gone, but the worlds with angels will rejoice, you will have grief and harrassment, but it will turn to joy after you are dead.

I have made known to you what to expect an all things before it takes place. Elijah is having his rest ill wake him up after death of this body (Adam) to begin his work on earth.

CHRIST (Adam) could hear the noise of the horses racing towards his nation and asked all his people to return to their homes and stay inside an dont come out and be observant.

Judah and his battalion of soldiers arrived in the holy nation in the night and waited for daybreak. The soldiers went in the nation and shouted Adam come forth every One stayed inside their home looking, the soldiers shouted Adam come outside, Prince Judah want to see you.

Adam walked slowly and stood before Judah and his soldiers naked, Judah looked at him fiercely with hate. CHRIST in the body Adam looked at judah and his soldiers, Judah asked; Where is Adam house, show me? Adam said I am, why did you come here with a battalion of soldiers dressed in a coat with many colours? Is it to do battle with me? Judah held Adam by his beard and said I want you to show me where CHRIST is or Ill kill you if you dont.

CHRIST said through the mouth of Adam! I am before you as an old man, who you want to kill. Judah said I want you to hand over all your people in your nation to me as a gift to the devils. CHRIST/Adam said; I cant do that, all my people is from my flesh am sorry and is in the hand of Elijah for holy work.

Judah said; If you are not willing to hand over your your people to me, I shall cast your body in a pit where no one see you or hear you crying. I set before you this day life or death. CHRIST/Adam said, its your desire to do me harm a Man in the presence of CHRIST who has done you no harm.

Judah said; Come follow me up the high ground by the tree and ill tell you what is in my heart to this day. Through the mouth of Adam CHRIST said, who do you think you are to speak to me this way, you are arrogant and have no respect.

It is the same arrogance god your father spoke to me and left the earth with you concieved in my daughter to be adopted, he is sorrowful for what he did to my daughter to make a god to be wicked like him. You are doing the same ordering me by the law of devils to come up to a tree with you with no fruit.

Whose god have I slain, or whose godly daughter have I taken away captive to fornicate or opress under oath? Who have I decieved to recive a bribe, which god have I brought up from birth tell me? CHRIST is witness.

Judah said; CHRIST is witness before my battalion of soldiers, Adam you have done none of tthese things. CHRIST (Adam) said Judah, Elijah adopted you, consider the way he brought you up from birth and forbid you should be against CHRIST.

If you do any wickedness to my people or me you shall be condemned to Death. When the soldeirs herd this they said prince Judah who is this? Judah got angry held Adam by his beard and pushed him.

CHRIST (Adam) kept his cool and said, Judah why have you come here in a peaceful nation with your battalion of gods with bow and arrows? Why did Satan choose you come here he is a murderer like god your father its Satan who strangled him to Death.

CHRIST (Adam) said, Judah its the devils you should be against for what they do to your mother under oath in captivity, But it is in your heart to do me harm, you know nothing about battle.

Judah said you are old and inferior to devils, the devils hate Christ and Elijah, I dont think Elijah and Christ will come and save you and all your people they will be extinct and gods will populate the earth for devils.

Christ (Adam) said; The devils and gods will be removed from the earth Judah so stop boasting in front of your soldiers, Elijah will come and throw you in the pit to be with god your father. Judah said I am sent by Satan to kill you, and Ill chalenge Elijah for the earth when I am a godly spirit.

THOU SHALL NOT TEMPT THE LORD

Judah said Adam you and your people live in hope CHRIST will save you from devils. CHRIST (Adam) said, its the third time I ask you to go and tell the devils to come and fight me but you insist to be the the first god to cast the first stone on my body. Your battalion of gods will be witness for the gods on earth if you do me harm. Juhah said I hope to be a king after I kill you.

CHRIST (Adam) said; You secretely envy Satam, he made gods with your mother and you are afraid if you dont kill me, what he will do to you. You are decietful and in fear of Satan if you dont do as he command.

THE UNLEAVEN BREAD

Judah said, Adam my soldiers have been riding for days without food they are hungry, if you belive in this illusive CHRIST put CHRIST to the test, make him feed my soldiers with bread from the sky.

THE gods SHALL NOT LIVE BY BREAD ALONE

CHRIST (Adam) said through the mouth of Adam, Judah make your soldiers sit on the grass and sit with them. I am going a stone throw from you and watch.

LET YOUR LIGHT SHINE BEFORE gods SO THEY CAN SEE YOUR GOOD WORK

The sun began to shine on the body (Adam) very bright, it dazzled the gods, CHRIST lifted the arms of adam toward the sun and commanded bread to fall from the sky, and suddenly bread began to fall on the grass by the soldiers, the soldiers picked up the bread and eat.

BLESSED ARE THOSE WHO MORN

EVE came with an alabaster box with ointment and said, Judah what has my MAN done to you? You come with soldiers to kill Adam. The soldiers began to laugh at this old naked WOMAN and said go back.

Christ (Adam) said to the soldiers, leave her alone, she came to anoint my body before before you kill me, you will always have Judah with you. Judah after my body is dead, tell Satan Eve anointed my body before you throw it in the pit, to remind him of god your father he strangled to take your mother in captivity with you.

Eve returned to her people crying, Judah is going to kill Adam, what have I done? Cain and Judah are merderers for devils on the earth.

CHRIST (Adam) said; Judah its better satan had eaten you from birth, Judah said I wont eat your flesh nor will I drink your blood, CHRIST (Adam) said you are in my flesh and it will cover the earth after my body is dead.

Judah said; Today you will be in the same chamber with god my father for giving Elijah his kingdom. I hate Elijah in my fathers image.

CHRIST (Adam) said, you hate Elijah who brought you up from birth and hate Christ you have not seen, and love Satan who held your mother captive with you in her womb. Judah got angry told the soldiers to put the hood over the head of Adam, and he he began to curse F . . . ing this and that who it is that slap thee tell us.

PARADISE LOST, THE PASSOVER

Judah said, Adam, tell me who is this CHRIST and I will let you go, CHRIST (Adam) said, if I told you. You will not belive and if I asked you who is ELIJAH you will not answer me before your soldiers, I am contented, Christ is my hand And my eyes and will suffer till my body is dead so Satan your king can reign by force and boast he distroyed Adam and Eve in paradise on earth. If you touch any of my people, Elijah will have no mercy on you an sprits from your seed.

CURSED IS HE WHO HANGED ADAM ON A TREE

The soldiers brought a colt among their horses, they put Adam on its back, took a rope made a noose and put it around Adam, s neck and tied the end to the branch on the Tree. Judah said; Adam, what is your last word? CHRIST (Adam) asked, is it lawful to save an innocent MAN or kill him?

You are a prophet to the gods to live to Death, if you steal or fornicate with any of my daughters in my nation woe is unter you for disobediance. All godly sprits in my flesh will face Death it will be justified to remove godly spirits from the earth from my flesh through ELijah when CHRIST is on his throne in haeven.

THE BODY OF CHRIST IS HANGED ON A TREE
2Pet 2 19-24

Judah got angry, took the rod in his hand and hit the colt. It jumped and went foreward and left the body Adam hanging on the TREE. Judah said to his soldiers, let us wait to see if CHRIST or ELIJAH will come and snatch his body from us. The body went limp and the SPIRIT CHRIST sepparated from his body and CHRIST was on his way to do battle against King devil of Death and devils in the ancient worlds.

The soldiers took the body of CHRIST (Adam) off the TREE, an put the dead body put on the colt and rode off, when they got in a valley. Judah took the body off the colt and threw it in a pit, then took big stones and threw it on the body, Judah and his battalion rode back to their nation.

The people of Christ Adam went to the TREE where the body of CHRIST was hanged after the soldiers left and they began to cry they carved on a stone, Cursed is he who hanged Adam on the TREE and they returned to their homes. Eve cried Elijah save me my Spirit I dread what the devils will do on earth.

THE PALACE OF SATAN

Judah went to the palace of satan, entered his chamber and said Adam is dead. Satan took a ring off his finger and put it on the finger of Judah, then took off the chain from his neck and put it around Judah's neck and said thanks an said now you shall be second in command after me.

THE ENTRANCE OF THE ANCIENT WORLDS

CHRIST left earth for the ancient world in darkness, when He arrived at the entrance, the receptionest asked who are you? You dont look like the Eternal who sent my King and devils back to our worlds in the dark.

CHRIST said; I am the son of the ETERNAL, my visit is to put the the worlds in the universe in order for peace and harmony. The receptionist said; King devil of Death is chained by Satan and every devil here is afraid to unchain him, why did the ETERNAL send you? Satan is not here, he went on a mission to earth to make godly sprits, he would be delighted to see you in our world.

The goddess is crying for Satan, he left her for the woman on earth, now you are in my world you cant get out, only the goddess Know the exit, if she let you out send Satan to her. She boast only Satan can satisfy her. While you are here do not unchain King devil of Death, he is malicious and hateful he has spread all the disease of Death to all devils to pass on his seed with Death.

THE DEVILS IN THE CHAMBER OF DEATH

The receptionist asked CHRIST; What is your purpose to be here before I let you in the chamber?

CHRIST said the devils on earh have broken the covernant with the ETERNAL they had no respect for holy Angels, Satan have commited rape with my woman to make a god an his god has slain my SON and raped my daughter to make a god to be like him on earth.

Satan kidnaped my daughter to make gods in her flesh, Satan and his devils had the son of god to hang My body on a tree and threaten my people with extinction from the earth to take the kingdom by force to make godly sprits on earth.

CHRIST went on to say, I an here to make the covernant between the Eternal and devils when they were in heaven obsolete to establish a new covenant for all angels the ETERNAL created by the WORD with everlasting life to live with my Sprits from the earth in peace an harmony with without Death, devils, godly sprits and darkness in the universe forever after Salvation in Kingdoms from my flesh.

The receptionist said; I fear if you get out of our world you will be a danger, an want to judge all devils and send us back to Death in the fire for ever, I surgest you go and see if there is a chamber in the maze open and wait on the goddess and Satan to deside your fate.

IN THE MAZE

CHRIST began to search in the labyrinth of tunels searching for King devil chained in the chamber. In the first chamber CHRIST saw a door, He broke the seal and opened the door an saw many devils inside the dark chamber The devils saw CHRIST in the LIGHT standing by the door, they began to scream in fear and asked what you want? Its not time to return to Death in the fire. CHRIST closed the door and sealded it.

CHRIST looked around in the maze of tunels and saw, a second chamber. He opened the door and a devil came towards CHRIST furiously and missed, CHRIST could see him, but the devil could not see Him as his LIGHT was to bright for his eyes. The devil fled in the darkest part and swang a chain at CHRIST it missed, CHRIST grabed the the chain and chained him, then closed the door and sealded it.

Christ went deeper into the labyrinth an saw a third chamber. The door was sealed like the previous two. CHRIST broke the seal an entered the chamber, an inside was King devil of Death the most vicious devil in the ancient world.

King devil shouted, what do you want? Satan chained me before he went to your worlds in the light. CHRIST said; I am CHRIST SON of the ETERNAL who sent Satan an all his devils back to your worlds for declaring war on his angels He created in HIS worlds in the light.

EVERLASTING LIFE AGAINST EVERLASTING DEATH

King devil asked, why did the ETERNAL send you? Is it to take the goddess with you? All I get from her is insults while I am chained. Set me free, I am in fear of what Death will do to me if I do not populate the worlds with devils. He has passed on his power to me. King devil said CHRIST if you are the SON of the ETERNAL with everlasting life with power, I am the son of Death with everlasting power of death. Let us put our power to the test. Everlasting Life against everlasing Death. King of devils said, CHRIST if you win you have more power to take the ancient worlds from me to be the new ruler of the universe.

CHRIST said; To the king of devils Death has broken the covenant of peace and harmony with the ETERNAL, by making you his first devil to rule the all worlds for Death with devls from his seed your son Satan came to earth and raped my Woman to make a god, and his god raped my daughter to make a god. Satan kidnaped my daughter while she was pregnant for god.

The son of god hang my body on a tree that is why I am here to send every devil back to Death begining with you who made a covenant with Death to return every devil and godly sprits from your seed back to Death. To remove your wickedness in the ancient worlds to establish a new covenant for peace and make the covenant between the

ETERNAL and devils obslete. By a new Testament to regain Paradise after every godly sprit is removed from my flesh.

THE BATTLE TO RULE THE UNIVERSE FOR ETERNAL LIFE OR DEATH

CHRIST took one look at the chains that bind king devil of Death an the chain came appart, king devil came at CHRIST with great force. Christ fell to the ground. As CHRIST was geting up on his feet, king devil came at CHRIST with full power of Death and butted Him on his head. Christ fell backwards he laughed get up, I am in the world before you.

The king took a heavy bar to hit CHRIST. CHRIST held on to the bar and both the king and CHRIST was puting their strength and power to the test. CHRIST overpowered him and took the bar and throw it aside. King devil managed to escape through a secret door in the chamber with four beasts guarding the chamber.

THE FOUR BEASTS

Christ found the secret door an saw the king with four beasts. King devil let loose oneof the beast, it had four heads with eyes in front and back and started coming with fire from its nostrils and smoke from its mouth roaring to attack CHRIST. The chamber began to echo with noise. The king shouted kill CHRIST.

CHRIST kicked the dust on the ground and it became fies and the flies began to go in the eyes of the beast and it couldn't see CHRIST and be came useless. The king let loose the next beast he called hate, an shouted kill, kill. The beast was ferocious and breathing out smoke and fire as it got close. CHRIST kicked the dust on the ground an it became flies, and the flies blocked the eyes of the beast an went up its nostrils, the beast began to roar in pain.

The king let loose the other two beasts and said attack CHRIST, they were in fear of CHRIST, seeing the other beasts roaring in pain, CHRIST took one look at them an they turned round to attack king devil he ran out of the chamber to the main chamber where all the devils were, an began shouting breathlessly CHRIST is here to send us to Death.

The devils began to scream, O king dont let CHRIST in here. The devils cast out of the worlds in the light were with the goddess, King devil got jelous and held the goddess by throat, you fucking bitch; You see this bastard Satan of yours has brought CHRIST here to send us in the fire to Death.

The ETERNAL, who you devinely praise pass judgment on Death for making you and I to populate devils. The ETERNAL sent all devils back to our worlds for tresspasssing in his worlds, now HIS CHRIST want to cast out devils from our world because Satan went to his world an rape his woman to make a god to hang his body. CHRIST is here to take vengence on devils begining with us for tresspassing on earth to make gods to polute his flesh with disease of Death.

The goddess cried, O king I warned Satan to leave the woman alone, she is a temptation an will bring alot of troble to devils if he made a god with her. The devils cast out of heaven with satan said; O king this CHRIST and his Elijah are slipery, they work according to a new testament in the tabernacle and we do not know what they will do to devils.

They work with a new system, one look after the other with a WORD that can penitrate any where in the universe. They are out to rule and have dominion in every world, O king let us hold CHRIST here and chain HIM here so we dont end in the fire with Death.

Another devil said; O king let the goddess go out to seduce him to see where he has his power and you can bring the worlds in the light back to darkness. the godess left and went to her chamber in fear of king devil.

THE THRONE IN HEAVEN IS THE PRIZE

Christ found the secret door to the main chamber and opened it, The devils saw CHRIST standing in the Light looking at them they were in great fear, Christ said all of you come forward ill show you my power, slowly they began to come forward, Christ put his hands up, they looked up to his outstreched hands to the Eternal, CHRIST kicked the switch and it released the trap and all the devils fell in the pit and all the devils journed to the gates of hell to be with Death.

CHRIST took a rest after casting all the devils in the pit. The goddess came out from her chamber and saw CHRIST asleep, she began to do enchantment to seduce Him to deep sleep. Where Elijah was having his rest on earth began to shake regorously he woke up and said wake up my LORD. CHRIST came out of his sleep. The goddess said; SON of the ETERNAL you have won the victory over King devil of Death.

Their are many kinds of disease from Death you have to conquer before you leave this world to be on the throne with victory. I am the mother of king devil with Death and have given birth to all devils with my king to pass on the seed of Death with disease to conquer the worlds. Satan and the other devlls left here will bring disease of Death in flesh of the woman on earth stay with me, and ill be satisfied.

CHRIST said I can not take you to earth with me, you will contaminate all my flesh with disease of Death. The goddess said; The ETERNAL saved me from the pit you threw my king and the devils. CHRIST dont leave me here alone, Satan is on earth making gods with your daughter. According to the covenant king devil and myself have with Death, if we fail to be king and queen and multiply devils to conquer the worlds he want every devil an all godly sprits from his seed to return to him.

I let Satan and 200 devils out by the exit to earth thinking he would populate the earth with godly sprits to conquer the worlds so we could rule as king and queen when he brought back the world in darkness, while king devil was chained now you want to leave me here and get out by the exit to earth.

CHRIST said; I will not harm you, ill leave you here in peace. The goddess said if you left me here Ill not see you again, what you did to king devil was justified because he was cruel and shut me in a dungean and sent many devils as an offering to Death to satisfy his lust. Now Satan is on earth with your daughter populating the earth instead of me, and Im here with you. The ETERNAL gave me visions of the new worlds in the light dont leave me here.

CHRIST said to the goddess; The problem is you are no damned good and corrupt as much as Death, the both of you wanted to rule the worlds in the universe with disease of Death to prevent the ETERNAL from ruleing his part of the universe in the light, you allowed your intense lust for Satan corrupt your plan to rule with him with gods instead of king devil and devils with you. Both you and Satan are corrupt an cant leave above worlds.

The ETERNAL made a covenant with Satan and other devils to live in peace and harmony and not to fornicate with angels or any of His creation to make a god to suffer in the fire with Death. It is a immortal Sin to make a god with the ETERNAL's creation. CHRIST went on to say, goddess if you did not let Satan out of the exit to earth, he would not come to earth to rape my woman to make a god to pass on the seed of Death to contaminate my flesh with disease. You conspired with Satan to make gods to be better looking than devils with King devil.

The ETERNAL created ZION as my Queen to rule with Me and Pass righteous justice from the throne in heaven on all devils if any devil made a god with his creation for all to live the Everlasting Death. For all angels to live in the worlds in peace and harmony. So goddess I will leave you here alone so I continue my work from the throne in heaven.

DISEASE OF DEATH

The godess became jelous of ZION who will rule as QUEEN of the Universe and not she, and was ashame of her conspiracy to rule the universe as queen with Satan as her King was not any more a secrete, she said before you and your Queen ZION have Victory over Death in this ancient world you must conquer all disease of Death before you rule on the throne. You have to pass the immune test to pass judgment on me.

She began to spew death of Cancer, death of Leprosy and all kinds of disease from Death on CHRIST, when their was no more disease to come out from her mouth she collapsed and fell then went to her chamber. CHRIST was imune to all disease of death.

THE EXIT TO EARTH

CHRIST did his holy work an shut the exit of the ancient world to earth an took a rest. The goddess came from her chamber and saw CHRIST resting, she said to her self Ill seduce him like I seduced Death to sire a good Spirit.

The earth began to tremble where Elijah was resting, he woke up and said the WORD and CHRIST woke up and saw the goddess doing enchantment over Him. CHRIST said you corrupt bitch what are you doing. She said its only you and I left in this ancient world come with me in my chamber and give me a Spirit like you before you go to your throne in heaven.

CHRIST said I shall not commit adultry. I love ZION she is my queen it would be a immortal sin if I made a spirit with you. You are corupt not holy pure. You are of from Death. She cried, CHRIST dont leave me here to be torn appart by the two beasts of king devil left in the ancient world they will tear me appart.

ENTER THROUGH THE NARROW GATE THAT LEAD TO HADE

CHRIST said goddess my work in the ancient world is finished with righteous judgment on king devil and the devils with only you left.

There is alot of work to be done to establish the kingdoms of gods for salvation to create Sprits with everlasting life to be accepted by the ETERNAL

Goddess! Salvation is far off, will you take the job as a receptionist at the entrance of Hades? She said to do what? CHRIST said its no good for you to be alone with these beasts when you can have more time with Satan before the final judgment come on devils on earth for rape.

You can take the book of Death with you and every godly sprit that go through the gates of Hades you can take their names to give to Death as they are all from his seed according to the covernant you and king devil have with him to return sprits from his seed back to him. She said you have given me two choices is either I stay with the two beast of king devil or enter the names of godly sprits of Satan and devils without flesh of zion an your daughter to Death in the Everlasting fire.

She accepted, ill be receptionist to take the names of godly sprits so I can spend more time with Satan and the devils until the final judgment before Salvation begin in kingdoms from Zion flesh.

CHRIST said; Before I let you out to journey to Hades, this is the covernant Ill have with you. Elijah will be the judge to give you and king devil every godly sprit that has no faith in Him and anti CHRIST on the days of Salvation, until salvation end with no godly sprits in the flesh of ZION and JERUSALEM, to be as it was in the begining with no gods on earth. The goddess was let out and was directed by the Spirit of the Sun to Hades.

FROM THE ANCIENT WORLDS CHRIST JOURNEY TO EARTH

CHRIST put new shuters to the entrance to hades for Satan and godly sprits to enter to await final judgment, and set up bands in the earth to absorb shock set up the north and south Portal for the wind to make clouds over the earth for the time of salvation to create Sprits in the kingdoms of gods after removing godly sprits to face judgment.

Christ set up the water course for water to flow through out the earth for vegetation, He set up hades in the bowel of the earth to be in fire with smokers to release the heat in the sea, He set up portholes for the wind to blow on the ice to bring, frost, snow and rain to cool the earth and to make mist in the time of salvation.

CHRIST set up the work to bring the four winds on earth, for Elijah to do his holy work in Judgment on devils and godly sprits an the resurection of Sprits by the WORD. After CHRIST finished His work he left the goddess in hades with the book of Death to take count of the devils she let out of the ancient worlds to return to Death, and also to take the names of godly spirts that enter hades, weigh them to know how much flesh of the daughters of CHRIST an ZION flesh that is used to make gods on earth be fore they enter their chamber to wait for final judgment to return to Death.

THE JOURNEY TO EARTH FROM HEAVEN

Eve went looking for the body (Adam) an met Elijah, she began to cry O, Elijah Im looking for the body of CHRIST I dont know where Judah and his battalion hid Adam. Elijah took her to the pit where the body was. Ark angel Michael came on a chariot with horses and waited on the cloud over the pit.

Elijah went inside the pit and brought up the body of CHRIST, it had no smell, or was going rotten holy pure. Ark angel Michael came down from the cloud with the carriage of horses to the pit said! Elijah I came for the body of CHRIST to put inside the tabernacle for all angels in the future to see the body of CHRIST as a testimony, before He sit on throne in heaven as the new creator of Sprits from the earth. Elijah put the body (Adam) inside the carriage. Ark angel Michael went back to the Cloud and Elikah said the WORD and the Four winds came unto the cloud and took the carriage with michael to the heavens with Adam. Eve began to cry. Elijah said Eve when you resurrect you will see Adam in the tabernacle to remind you when you and Adam was in the flesh.

THE THRONE IN HAEVEN

The throne in heaven was built before Christ and Zion was created in the body of ADAM, The ETERNAL prophysied after he took his rest what Christ will do before Christ sit on the magnificent throne he would dispence justice, and have power authority to rule and have dominion in all worlds according to the testament in the ark in the tabernacle.

To execute justice and judgmaent to establish the Kingdom under a new testament to create New Sprits to populate the worlds with Sprits with everlastig life through Elijah with the WORD on the days of Salvation of kingdoms.

JESUS JOURNEY FROM HEAVEN TO EARTH

The angels in heaven were waiting for the victory of CHRIST against King devil of Death and his devils in the ancient world in the darkness.

Jesus came from heaven with a cariage with white horses and waited on the cloud for CHRIST to come from the ancient world to the earth. Suddenly Christ submerged from the deep and began to walk on air to where Zion (Eve) and Elijah was, Eve looked up an saw Jesus in the cloud She said Elijah look Jesus is in the Cloud.

Suddenly CHRIST appeared an came towards EVE and Elijah, Eve tried to hold Him CHRIST said not now, you are still in your image, return to our children and tell them you saw me and Im on my way to heaven to prepare a place for them and you and I to rule and have dominion in all worlds.

CHRIST said! Elijah I love you My Son! Elijah said I know that my holy Father, CHRIST said! Elijah save Zion and all your Brothers and Sisters SPRITS and resurrect them to ME on the throne in heaven all is in your hands. You are the judge over all on earth, to execute justice an righteous judgment on devils an gods who harm them.

Christ began to walk on air towards the cloud to meeet Jesus waiting for him in the clouds with a carriage with horses. CHRIST and Jesus met and embrace each other, it was the first time they met since Jesus separated from the dead body of Abel. Jesus The first Sprit of Christ and Zion to resurrect and returned to take up Christ his Father to the Throne in heaven. They waved to Zion EVE and Elijah and went inside the carriage.

The ETERNAL said through the cloud to CHRIST. MY Son I love come up to the Throne prepared for you to sit with dignity, honour, in magesy to rule with power and have dominion in all worlds with righteous judgment.

There was clapter in heaven with shouts of Halelujah CHRIST Death has no Power over thee, their was thunder and lightning in the cloud Elijah commanded the four winds to come unto the Cloud and take Christ and Jesus to the throne in heaven.

When CHRIST and Jesus got to heaven, the angel began to blew teir horn to welcome CHRIST, and began to sing CRHIST has the victory over Death and took the worlds of King devil of Death for ever, they began to sing woe woe woe to the devils an godly sprits on earth. The kingdoms on earth are for SPRITS of CHRIST. Reign for ever.

The angels began to sing! Hail Elijah judge the devils an their godly sprits those who have no faith in you and anti Christ, return them to Death after you pass judgment on Satan and devils for making gods to pass on the disease of Death.

THE TESTAMENT IN THE ARK. Ps146.10. Ps93.1Ps98.1

CHRIST sat on the throne! Twenty four rulers of other worlds came and prostrate on their knee and bow their head on the floor before Him and said, we give you praise CHRIST LORD Of the ETERNAL for your victory over king devil of Death. You are worthy to rule all worlds from your throne with power to create SPRITS with Everlasting life on earth from your Throne in Heaven through your Son Elijah with the WORD.

Then came rumbleing of thunder, The Eternal commanded lightning to break the seal on the ark in the Tabernacle to take out the scroll of the prophysy of what CHRIST would do before He sat on the Throne in heaven.

Jesus took the scrol and read out what the ETERNAL testified what CHRIST would do before he sat on the Throne to make the covernant with Satan and devils while they were in heaven among angels in heaven obsolete, so angels in heaven can live by the new Testament by CHRIST without darkness, Death, devils and godly sprits forever after the final judgement.

ELIJAH KING OF THE EARTH

The angels began to sing, O Elijah you are worthy to have the WORD to be king of the earth to bring glory to Sprits CHRIST will create in Kingdoms for Salvation, so the Sprits created can continue in the kingdom to populate the earth with SPRITS to be with us in heaven.

After Jesus read out the prophysy of the ETERNAL, the multitude of angels in the Tabernacle came to the throne an gave CHRIST praise for His victory over Death with righteous Judgment over devils of Death an worthy to sit on the Throne as the New CREATOR of Sprits in Kingdoms from His flesh for Salvation. The Angels shouted, hallelujah Salvation and power has come to CHRIST the CREATOR to reign and have dominion in all worlds in the universe according to the new testament.

THE PASSOVER

Zion (Eve) gathered her people in the tabernacle; and said, my children I have seen the Sprit of CHRIST your Father and also your brother Jesus, he was waiting in the cloud to take Him to heaven. Before He met Jesus He told me he is going to prepare a place for us in heaven.

Eve said, remember what CHRIST said while he was in His body (Adam) do not be afraid of devils and gods who will kill you and cant kill your Sprit, if and devil or god come in our nation to attack you, use restraint and suffer death of your body so your Sprit can enter heaven as innocents who has harmed no one on earth.

Judah dishonoured me before he hanged the body of CHRIST, when I sit as Queen in heaven I will see judgment on him and god his father for rapeing your sister and conspireing with the devils to hold your sister in captivty.

Zion (Eve) said, my children have faith in Elijah to save your Sprit, after you leave your body you shall sleep till Elijah wake you to resurrect to heaven to be with your Father. At the moment we are like sheep for slaughter, so every one of you prepare yourselves for death of your body.

Eve said hold on to your Faith in Elijah for your Sprit to live the Eternal life among angels in heaven and not the life on earth with gods and devils who will always be against you and want to fight you because you are accepted in heaven and not them. They will want to fight you till you perish from the earth.

Eve said; Elijah will execute judgment on all the devils on earth if they harm us. When Eve was through speaking the congregation in the tabernacle they said Amen, and returned to their homes confident and put their life in the hand of Elijah to do His holy work to resurrect them to heaven.

THE PUNISHMENT OF QUEEN TAMUZE

Satan invited the kings to his palace, one of the kings said, Satan their is a rumour going around, Satan said what is the rumour? The gods want Judah to be a king. Another king said, Satan Judah is always drunk and is cruel like king devil to the gods in his battalion and they are in fear of him.

Satan said, I hoped when he went to hang Adam, Adam would kill the bastard and we would have reason to say Adam murdered our god to take revenge. One of my princes saw Tamuze leaving his house drunk late in the night, Satan got vex and called the eunuchs and said prepare the Queen and bring her to the brazen altar in the santuary and also tell the scribe to come and take note what I am going to do for future generation of gods.

When Queen Tamuze came she said what do you want with me with the kings? Satam said ill tell you what I want. One of the kings began to curse, you fucking whore filled with the disease of death poluting yourself with Judah.

Satan said, Judah is going to kill your brothers, I am going to make giants then you will see who you will fuck with in the palace. Tamuze began to cry, O king have mercy, if you kill my brothers there will be none left on earth, kill the gods instead they are always sick with the disease of Death. Satan said who are you to tell me what to do well you made them with disease of Death.

Tamuze answered the seed you put in my womb is full of disease from death to make gods to perish with your deciet. My body will never go to heaven, nor will I suffer after its dead, death is unto my body every day in this palace, I want to die so I can be free of this oath and you will not have it to fuck. Satan I am bored being your queen, you hold me incaptivity with your false vision to bring the worlds back to darkness with godly sprits.

A king said, Satan she is getting smart, you should not teach her to speak in our tongue, she has no respect for you and I fear in your vexation, if you put your hand and on the mother of gods, Elijah will come after us.

Satan said this whore make me jelous, she torment me with her words, ill eliminate her brothers from the face of the earth for fucking with Judah. I put this creature in my palace and now he is fucking my queen and boast to the gods he has a great secret no devil know until he become a king of gods.

QUEEN TAMUZE CHASTIZE SATAN

Queen Tamuze said to Satan you can never satisfy my body, you will go to hell for it; Satan said ill kill your ass if its the last thing I do on this earth, Tamuze said kill me you coward or tell the murderer of my Father to do it for you. My body is no good it has become disease from you. Set it on fire to ashes.

Satan said to the kings; you always have lust for my queen, you can put all the abomination of Death in her

The first King began to f . . . . k and curse her, she was in much pain and sore, another king took his turn and began f . . . k and call her bitch, whore an she began to cry bleeding, another king took his turn, she cried you bastard devil kill me, another took his turn and he began to swear you f . . . k this and that, the pain was intense and unbearable he said repent for fucking with Judah, She said I would rather die than repent to you F . . . kers.

Another king took his turn and started swearing mother f . . . . ker repent, She cried kill my body so I can be Free from this oath with your abuse, Satan took his turn and went into her with vengence for tormenting him with her words and nearly tore her appart saying, you f . . . ing whore, prostituted with the kings on earth.

She answered, now Elijah have reason to cast all of you from the earth for your filth in holy flesh and ill be free forever when you are no more on earth according to the oath. Elijah will judge all of you for what you did to my body.

Satan told the eunuchs to put Tamuze in the dungeon. The scribe wrote queen Tamuze mother of gods prostituted herself—with the kings of devils.

AFTER THE ABOMINATION OF THE KINGS

The kings got together to deside on a plan; Satan said I fear Elijah will come and take revenge for our abomination, Let us all agree on this plan to kill all the Sons of Adam so His seed perish from the face of the earth for our gods to populate godly sprits, to succeed with our plan before Elijah come to remove us from the earth.

Satan called the eunuchs and said; Tell Queen Tamuze to come to my chamber to make supplecation to me for her brothers, a decree has been passed by all the kings to make her Brothers extinct from the face of the earth an She should come to my chambers to make supplecation to me for her Brothers.

Tamuze put on her royal clothes of fine linen, scarlet purple pink, amulets and gold tinkle bells on her feet, put on Satans favorite parfume and came to his room, took off the vail from her face and said; do you want to kill me king or commit more abomination? As you can see I am still alive, so kill me, treat yourself to my death so I will be with my Brothers you want to extinct from the earth.

Satan said; You f . . . ing bitch do you want to know why I have not invited you in my bed chamber up to this day?

Tamuze said it doesn, t realy matter, the sooner my body is dead the better, Satan asked so where is your fear? Creatures of the earth dont live for ever. Tamuze said one night pleasure with my body is not enough, kill me so my body can be dead like a creature on earth.

Satan said; My fear is not in you anymore. Your body is like a snare unto me. You are a creature that is here today an gone for ever. Did you come in my bedchamber to mock me. You use to trembleing and ask for mercy in my bed before, now you speak boldly, dont ever think you will escape death in this palace.

Tamuze said when you took me in captivty I was pregnant for god (cain) and I was in fear of you and what you would do if it was a son of god, your wickedness is unbearable, you hanged my Father and now you want to make my brothers extinct from the earth to populate gods.

THE TIME HAS COME FOR DEVILS TO TAKE THE KINGDOM BY FORCE

Satan said to Tamuze I want to make myself clear to you, I am going to multiply gods in this palace with your Mother and sistes, after your Brothers perish from the earth I dont care if you are dead. Now what is your request before all your Brothers vanish like mist from the earth.

Tamuze said; O king of nations with so many of my sisters to f . . . k, you will be weak like king devil you chained in the ancient world, you will have no power left in you to fight against Elijah an CHRIST. O king if you cant satisfy my body, how will you satisfy so many of my sisters, they are hard to please only my Brothers can satisfy them. Satan said what is that to you, you will be dead from disease from Death in your flesh.

Tamuze said; You will be ancient history if Judah or you slay my Brothers to take my sisters in captivity to satisfy your lust to establish your foolish vission to be the king of the world, Tamuze looked at him with pity and said when you make my brothers extinct you will see who is the King of the world.

TAMUZE PUT SATAN TO THE TEST

Satan looked at tamuze with love and hate. Tamuze said so you want to capture My Mother and sisters to polute their body with your filth from Death and want me to make supplication for my Brothers.

She walked slowly toward satan lying in bed, she stood, looked at him and began to undress slowly, took some parfume pored some drops in the palm of her hand and blew the parfume in his face, the scent went up his nostrils and all the hate he felt turned to lust. Satan said Im like a beggar to you in this bed and want to kill you if I dont F . . . k you.

Tamuze drew near him and blew more parfume in his face, he took out his big C and said touch it I beg you, in his excitement he said I will do any thing you request even half of the earth. Tamuze said kill me so the the flesh of gods be my inheritance on earth. My request O king; Let my body please thee till you are satisfied, my body is a burden to me I want to perish with my Brothers.

O king I hate what you do, Its abominable, I feel ashame of what I have to do for peace, for you and devils to leave My Father and Mother an brothes and sisters to live in peace to make gods in my flesh with you according to the oath. You keep me in captivity like a prisoner. My people have caused you no harm an if you kill them there will be no peace.

Tamuze went on to say, I am fed up of being a slave to you to make gods to pass on your seed to live unto Death. If I have satified thee O King stay in bed and ill prepare super for thee. Satan fell asleep.

Tamuze locked Satan in his room and secretly went to see Judah. She told him to keep away she has a plan for him to be king in the palace.

THE LAST SUPPER

Tamuze invited the kings to have super with Satan, she gained Satan confidence and during super Satan said to the kings, my queen, satisfy me now and she can have any thing even half the earth; Tamuze said; O king of nations Im in fear of Judah, let it be writen that Judah will not go with you to take my sisters and Mother so the gods in the future will know its recorded. Satan called for the scribe to write what Tamuze request. The scribe handed what Tamze requested to Satan, he sealded it with the ring on his finger an gave it to Tamuze.

Satan said; Tamuze it was in my heart not to bring Judah to fetch your sisters, I am afraid of him like you. Tamuze said he is an enemy to you o king whom I fear most. Satan left the table and went outside, he began walking up and down in the garden meditating on what he should do to have the victory on earth.

JEALOUSY AND FEAR OF DEATH

Fear of kidnaping all the women of CHRIST (Adam) and Zion (Eve) Satan meditated would give him the victory for the earth. to populate it with gods. Tamuze wants out to be free of the oath and eager to die I will have a choice with her people, Satan began talking to himself, if I dont go and fetch her sisters, Tamuze will call me a coward and say I am afraid of CHRIST an Elijah.

Satan said to himsef, Tamuze want me to go an fetch her Mother an sisters am afraid it will bring confrontation with CHRIST and Elijah. They are illusive and invisible to devils. So did Satan converse with himself. I want vengence, for casting me out of heaven, I feel hate an malice and afraid if I fail I will end in the fire with Death. I cant handle all this by my self, Judah has zapped power from me and want to be king of on earth.

Satan went back inside to join the the kings and Tamuze to finish supper, he could feel Judah, s hunger for power and felt humiliated the gods want him to be their king, Satan got vex for falling in love and being a slave to please a creature who has no fear of Death. He told the scribe to fetch Judah.

Judah came, he said; king of nations you asked for me, here I am as you requested. Satan took a good look at Judah, knowing the temptation to kidnap the women is risky, he took the ring from his finger and put it on the finger of Judah and said when I am not in the nation you are ruler of my palace and have authority over all gods.

Tamuze came and stood before Satan and the kings, said O king of nations I have a request, go and bring my people here to be with me and not send Judah, do me the favour O king, I cant endure to see the evil that will come unto them if Judah go and fetch them.

THE KINGS DEBATE TO TAKE THE KINGDOM BY FORCE

,A king said; Satan, I apologise, I was not in your palace to partake in the abomination with queen Tamuze, If Judah think he is worthy to be a king among us, let him prove he has faith to live unto Death like us according to the covenant with Death. Another king said; Satan, since Judah hanged Adam, CHRIST and Elijah have not attacked us, its time to to capture Eve and her daughters to populate gods, the gods we are making are always sick with cancer, rheumatism, gonorrhoea infecting each other with all kinds of disease in the flesh from Death.

Satan said; I intend to do a new kind of god to populate the earth with our giant devils but I am hesitant to capture the daughters of Eve, I am concious CHRIST and ELIJAH is up to something. Another king said; Satan, we cannot afford to take risk we cant return to heaven. One mistake an will be with Death for ever, an we will be the laughing stock, even gods will lauth at us living the good life in heaven an come to earth to make them with menstruous creatures on earth. The king went on to say the daughters of Eve are beautiful like angels in heaven. Satan these blessed women are a temptation to rape an make gods.

It is true Adam is no more among his people and this temptation to capture the women is a trap set for us to return to Death in the everlasting fire of Ammagedon.

Satan; replied, Death is the problem every devil have to face if we fail to rule on earth. According to the covenant with every godlysprit of gods from our seed will return to him in the fire for ever. Tamuze is not like our goddess who see things before it happens. If we fail to capture the earth our mother an Death will laugh at me and call me a foolish King with false hope, that is why we are gathered here brothers to debate to come to a mutual decision. So far so good, victory is in our grasp to rule on earth as Kings with our godly queens so we dont End in Fire to face Death an our mother.

Satan went on to say brothers I thaught if I got rid of Adam, his people would scater and be in fear of us, but they not afaid of devils though they know how wicked we are., My queen Tamuze is the same and have no fear of devils. She say her body will see no sorrow neither her dead body will shed tears for me. We devils are dealing with creatures as hard as granite rocks that will not split, I have to go down on my knee to satify my lust for her flesh, she laugh at me an say I cant satisfy her I am an old devil. You kings have godly women who are from the seed of Death. My Hebrew queen is in captivity under oath by force she is not like your godly queens from my seed.

Another king said; Satan, we dont seem to be going forward with your plan, we were cast out of heaven because you made a god with Eve, she is one of the ETERNALS creature He created on earth if we go and and capture her daughters with Adam its going to bring the final judgment on us on earth.

Satan; Replied we abandoned the covenant we had with the ETERNAL when we were in heaven not to make gods with his angels, now you are making gods from the flesh of His creatures on earth. You fuckers are happy with your godly women how can you say we have not achieved nothing because the sprits of gods cant go to heaven where we came from because the ETERNAL will not accept them?

The only way to achive anything is to populate the earth with gods to make godly sprits to pass on our seed to make gods to fight for the earth to remain earth bound if our plan fail. If we kill all the Sons of

Adam we will stop making holly people of the ETERNAL on earth to gain more time from the final judgment By Elijah.

A king said; Satan we surely have a proplem if we fail the gods will be fatherless as you can see, the gods will not want to associate them selves with us as their father an will want to worship kings Judah as their mighty God an King, they will say if we fail he is a god like them. Satan it seems we are not liked in heaven or by our gods on earth and should not come to earth, but we are here, so let us enjoy ourselves and be content with our queens, an be patient with your Hebrew queen the mother of gods who say she is not satified as long as you satisfy your lust.

Another king said; Satan, you say your queen is a menstruous creture you cant satisfy, how could we satisfy Angels in heaven? We devils lived under strict Statute an conditions of what we could not do in heaven. We knew to make a god is a immortal sin punishable like Death in the fire. We devils are accursed no matter where we live outside the boundry of the ancient worlds of darkness. Now our gods want Judah to be king of gods not knowing the Truth of Death.

Another King said; Satan, you see how ungrateful gods are, in front of us they are in fear of us, in our absense they will lie and cheat and boast its king Judah who created them and not us if you gave these fuckers a chance they will fuck their mother and say its the devil made them do it and not judah, gods will blame us for all their faults and disease from Death. That is why we should not trust them and capture the daughters of Eve to make giants to take over the earth and hope judgment dont come on us so we can see their future on earth.

Another king said; Satan, if gods want judah to be their king, what is the problem? he is a god that is skillful, you made him a prophet to teach gods,. he is ruthless as a devil an will make gods live by our covernant with Death.

Another king said; Satan, we have right to make gods according to the oath with your queen Tamuze for gods to live in her flesh until they are free from her flesh as godly sprits to live like devils to have lust for flesh, and corrupt it with disease of Death.

Another King said; Satan, as long as the people of Adam and Eve are on earth they are owners of the earth, they are free born and are exempt from living under the covenant we have with Death. If gods want Judah to be their king tell him to take a battalion of his soldiers and slay all the Sons of Adam so he can be a king among kings on earth.

SATAN AND THE KINGS CONFRONT JUDAH

The kings agreed they found a solution to their problem and invited Judah to the synagogue of Satan. Judah sat among the kings. Satan said; Judah the kings have been hearing the gods want you to be their king? What have you to say about this? We are old Kings from ancient worlds, I have promoted you to be the prophet to our gods to teach them what Death commanded to rule the world.

Now the gods want you to be their king on earth, Judah no god is as inteligent as you or wicked as you, if we make you a king with us you will have authority to govern to rule all all gods on earth as their king. We have no right to make laws on the people of Adam you hanged, I have made you a prince because you were born on earth, so would you like to be a king of the earth?

Judah replied O kings I have a desire to be a ruler, but if you want me to be a king of the earth, I will carry on doing your wickedness according to what Death command, to live by the laws of devils to Death though I hate what I have done to please you, and what ill have to do to be a king of gods on earth.

Satan said you cannot be a king of the earth while Sons of Adam are heirs of the earth, you have to Slay them all to be king of the earth.

JUDAH PUT THE FEAR OF CHRIST AND ELIJAH ON THE KINGS

Judah said to the devils; kings, when I hanged Adam for you, Adam said, if I killed any of his people, CHRIST and Elijah will come after me, you ask me to go and kill all the sons of Adam, if I did that I will be condemning myself and every god that came from my seed to Death.

Why dont you get your princes to slay them for you or slay them yourselves, I have a desire to be a ruler, but to be a king of the earth I might end in hades before you, surpose the Hebrews kill me I will be condemned to Death. Adam warned me if I touch any of his people CHRIST will come after me.

This put fear in Satan and the kings they shudered in fear and started to sweat. Satan said, Judah you are the most inteligent among gods, how else can you be a king with us if you dont Slay all the Sons of Adam? I made myself a king on earth by taking queen Tamuze the dauther of Adam incaptivity and force her to take the oath to make gods in her flesh. Now the gods want you to be their king, its by your wickedness you will be a king to rule our gods on the face of the earth.

One of the kings said; Judah when you came to the mountain with your herd you were like a wild beast satan accepted you and made you a prince after you agreed to take the oath to hate CHRIST an Elijah an made you a prophet to teach the gods to live under the commandment of Death. Now you are promoted to be a King. Now tell us what does Death command? Judah said;

Death command if we fail to give him the victory in the worlds he want every sprit we pass from his seed to return to him an that law apply to me and every god that pass on the seed from Death. Death commands all sprits from his seed to do all kind of wickedness, steal commit adultry, do wickednes to others, greed, depravity, disobey, and be ruthless to stop the CHRIST of the ETERNAL from ruleing all worlds.

Satan said Judah all this is in the law and its the covenant with Death and its inplanted in thee to be king on earth.

Judah said; O kings I know I am wicked, but all my wicked is not justified before Elijah, He will abandon me to Death If I murder innocent Sons of Adam to please you! I have no FAITH in Elijah, but the Sons of Adam have Faith in Him. If I go an slay the Sons of Adam,

Elijah will not let me rest in peace on earth and ill come face to face with Death. O kings I am accursed like you. All the kings went silent looking at Judah to make up his mind to be king of the earth.

Judah realize its his coice if he wants to be a king with the devils. The WORD with Elijah bring him back to his youth, Elijah saying to him go to the mountain an save your mother from the devils is ringing in his head. He blocked his ears, the voice of Elijah saying my WORD is good enough if you need help. The kings were stearing at him and was in fear of them if he said no to spilling blood of innocent sons of Adam, remembering the words of Adam if you touch my people CHRIST will come after you.

The kings looked at him strugling to say yes to be a king, no FAITH no Peace. The warning by Elijah I will abandon you, a warning by CHRIST/Adam before he hanged the body of CHRIST saying I will come after you all this spining in his head. He looked at the kings with hate an vengence for being born in wickedness of god his father (cain) rapeing his mother to pass on his accursed seed to him.

Every god born is accursed from the seed from death. Elijah warned him, when you are a godly sprit you will not accepted, only you body I will accept for salvation to present to the creation to be my SON in Craetion in your mothers flesh. Judah started to realise He needed Elijah to save him, he condemned himself hanging Adam for the devils because he had no FAITH in Elijah to rest in Peace and will face Death with the devils.

This was to much for Judah to handle he said, so be it, I have codemned my self, he looked at the kings and said I want to be a King, I will kill all to be a king on earth. The Satan and the Kings jumped and said now you are a king of Kings on earth to rule and share the victory with us on earth and they celebrated with King Judah.

PARADISE LOST

The kings got together to celebrate Paradise lost. Satan boasted; I will bring victory on earth to devils through king Judah, after Satan boasted how he will conquer the earth. A king said; Satan after King Judah slay all the Sons of Adam he will be condemned with us and all godly spirits of our gods on earth will return to Death, if they don have Faith in Elijah and Christ for peace.

Satan said; You keep talking of judgment you should be talking about captureing the Hebrew women to make giants to fight for the earth with us if CHRIST an Elijah come to Attack us on earth.

Another king said; Satan my godly queen had a dream and she saw much snow in one place, and much snow in another place with winds howling and saw our goddess with a book writing down names an saw in that place devouring flames of fire and she began to cry in her sleep.

Satan said; How you fuckers expect to have victory, if we dont spill blood of Adam and cut of his seed from from from populating holy people on earth. King Judah said; king of nations do you think CHRIST will be against gods in the flesh of the women for our wickedness for making the Sons of Adam extinct on earth.

Satan said; king judah you have submited to do like devils to be a king with supreme authority to punish the good people and silence any god who have faith in Elijah to rest in peace on earth, because Death will say sprits from his seed that has not returned to him is because they have FAITH in the saviour to rest in PEACE and he will punish us in the fire.

Satan went on to say our gods are born in flesh, an live unto Death an have a have a choice before they become godly sprits to have Faith in Elijah to save them after their body is dead. Elijah will return godly sprits to Death if they dont have no Faith in Him and its justified to return godly sprits who are ignorant of this choice. Faith for Peace or fall like us.

Satan went on to say the Hebrew women will know what is justified when they feel my anger an become our slaves to sin and make godly sprits to have dominion in their flesh to live according to the covenant with Death

Another king said; Satan, my queen dreamt about us being in a place with much fire in a watery place full of gloom and devils were crying for their queens, she was perspireing in her sleep an woke up cryin and afraid for me.

Another king said Satan; My queen had a vision and saw a Sprit in the light writing down names of the people of Adam, then she saw a Tempest came an took all the devils an she saw we began to fall on top of each other an we vanish. She began to cry in her sleep, Satan he said I am afraid this is a warning, the Women is a temptation for us to fall.

Satan said; how else can we have victory? The Hebrews are like nails in our eyes unless we slay all their men to vanish like mist there will always be temptation to capture their women. It is not that we dont like our gods we love our gods and fucking them is not a sin. But if we fuck holy women of Adam to make gods our gods will be born in sin from birth to populate gods to have the victory on earth.

Satan went on to say; According to the testament in heaven, Elijah's work is in salvation of kingdoms, He is not interested in gods, He will discriminate gods who has no Faith in Him, and look at them as shit on earth that has no right to pass on the seed of Death in the flesh of Adam an Eve. That is why king Judah is going to slay all the Sons from the oldest to a suckling just born, because he is not accepted as a Son of Adam.

THE FINAL JUDGMENT ON THE SONS OF ADAM

In the synagogue of Satan the kings gathered : Satan said I dont want to be the only one to pass judgment to slay the Sons of Adam, we must all swere this is mutuaally agreed by oath so if we fail Judgment will be justified on all of us to share the blame when we face Death for failing to give him the victory over the Eternal in the Light for the worlds in the universe.

A king said if I swear to this oath; King Judah must swear by this oath he shall not slay the women, nor fornicate with any of the daughters of Adan and Eve neither shall any god in his battalion or he shall no more be king of gods on the earth.

Satan said; King Judah take as many soldiers you have trained for battle and slay all the Sons of Adam to stop the seed of Adam from populating holy people on earth.

THE END OF THE SONS OF ADAM

Every family of the holy people of CHRIST/Adam and Zion/ was inside their houses singing and eating and incontrol, prepard for their hour to be dead for their Sprit to live the ever lasting Life, they knew holy scripture and prepared to sacrifice there body for this sabbath of their blood on earth.

King judah had his soldiers to sharpen their cutlass and spears then set out on horseback for a seven day journey to the holy land of Adam as they got closer to the Hebrews (So the devils called the holy people of Adam) the women could here the galoping noise of horses racing towards their nation.

When king Judah and and his battalion got to the holy land, his soldiers surrounded the nation with no wall with houses and no one in the streets. The soldiers began to shout, King Judah want to talk to the elder Son of Adam, come outside to talk with our king.

The elder Son came out and said what do you want? why do you come in the holy land of my Father with a battalion of soldiers in red and black uniform with cutlasses and spears? we have not fornicated with any god or hold any in captivity, nor have we stolen any thing from you or the devils, or harm any one or did anything wrong. So why are you here? If its bread and water you want, my family will be happy to give you?

King Judah looked at the elder Son, their eyes locked, Judah said to himself if I dot kill him, Satan will strangle me.

The elder Son said we are peaceful people and respect every one and expect the same so what is the reason for your visit? Elijah will not be pleased if you or your soldiers did harm any one? Judah asked where is he? Tell him to come to save you.

The elder Son said; I dont know where He is, He could be anywhere even looking at us as we speak I know when I see him again he will be sending me to a place where you cant come with your soldiers, so king Judah I suggest you return to the devils and tell them we have no war with you and your soldiers.

The elder Son went on to say; Judah what have my people done to you? did you come to remind us of the sin of god/Cain with my sister to make a god to come and mock us in front of your soldiers with arrogance and hate for people who did you no wrong.

You were also rude to Elijah who adopted you, brought you up, you thought was god your father. The last time Elijah was here, He said you turned against Him and became an anti CHRIST under oath to be a prophet to teach the gods of the devils the covennants with Death. Judah you are here with soldiers, we will not fight with you and your soldiers so please leave in PEACE.

NO FAITH, NO PEACE, FOR THE WICKED

The elder Son said; Judah if you slay any of my people, you will have no peace and shall be in danger of judgment. If you or any of your soldiers with cutlass an spears spill our blood on earth. To bring condemnation on all gods on earth for every droop of blood of my Father that is spilled. It will be justified when CHRIST remove all sprits of gods from His flesh on the face of the earth for Elijah to judge those who dont have Faith in him to rest in Peace.

Judah said Elder; If I open my mouth, you will be the first to be slain and you will perish like Adam who hoped Elijah would save him. I have lisoned to all you had to say, I hate Elijah in the image of god my fathers Kingdom, so tell all the men in their houses to come outside with their Sons, even those that suck the breast. I am the king of gods and all gods obey me, so tell all your brothers to come outside with their Sons.

IS IT LAWFUL TO KILL THE INNOCENT

The Elder Son said; Judah We are born free from laws of strangers go and tell satan and his devils so, but if its you desire to slay my people, CHRIST will come after you. The cock crowed.

Judah said, you have no respect for the king of gods with my soldiers, If I tell my soldiers to go inside the homes and cast out all the men from the oldest to the youngest the soldiers will slay them all the cock crowed a second time.

The Elder Son said, Judah you are threatening me and my brothers, if you or your soldiers slay any of my brothers you be condemning every god and they will live on earth untill CHRIST come to remove them in kingdoms, and where Elijah will put them, there is no bread and water because of your wickedness.

Judah said; Elder for the third time I command you to tell all your brothers to come outside with their Sons, If not you will be the first to be slain. The cock crowed the third time.

The Elder said; Judah it will be justified when Elijah speak through the mouth of you father to send you to a place where their is alot of ice and howling winds to cool your temper for sheding blood of the Son of my Father who has done you no wrong. CHRIST said vengence belong to him. Judah shudered at th thaught of ending in a place in freezing condition.

And went onto say did you come to murder me and my brothers then to rape our women after, like god your father to pass on the accursed seed of devils of Death. Their godly sprits will blame you for being born in Sin in the flesh of my sisters.

FAITH IN ELIJAH

The flesh of my Mother and my sisters is there inheritance on earth for ever. I am sure Elijah told you to have Faith in Him, for your Kingdom to be created to be a SPRIT like Him in Salvation to be his Son after your sprit depart from your mothers flesh so your sprit can rest in peace. Your mother's flesh is her inheritance on earth.

Judah if you commit abomination with any of my Sisters, to make godly sprits in their flesh. Elijah promised you, he will returned every godly sprit from you in the gate. Judah, you and your soldiers should be fighting devils for holding your Mother in captivity and not come to commit rape and murder.

REVELATION OF THE TRUTH

The Elder said; Judah when Elijah gave you the this promiss it was by himself and not by the law of devils, if you permit me to tell you the truth, god/Cain your father had no respect for my Father who brought him from birth, you have done the same and have no respect for Elijah who brought you up from birth. If Elijah was your Father you would love me and my Mother and Brothers an Sisters but you are the son of god who you do not know.

You were not born when god your father slay my Brother Abel/Jesus. You hanged my Fathers body on the tree an now you come here with your battalion of gods to slay the Sons of my Father who has done you no harm to be a king of gods on earth in conspiracy to rule with Satan and other kings of devils to populate gods to hide the truth of what you have done to my Father to lead gods astray with the false doctrin of devils, and also to hide your origin, to make gods belive you are a supper god self created in the world.

Judah, the Elder went on to say god your father was a deciver like you in your mother, s captivity. I know you dont want your soldiers to know the truth of your birth and who is your father, as Elijah explained he is in your fathers kingdom and he is not your father. Satan an the devils decieved god/cain also with false hope. Satan has done the same to you with false hope, and made you a Prophet to gods and a king if you to Slay the son of My Father. Also foryou to hate CHRIST AND Elijah.

THE EPELOGUE : THE HOUR HAS COME

The commander Of the soldiers said; King Judah we are commanded by the law any one on earth who love CHRIST and Elijah to slay them, the people of Adam dont like devils and our kings. We came here to slay the Sons of Adam an leave the women for the kings to deal with, so say the word to slay their men so we can return our nation.

The Elder Son of Adam said; Judah if you slay me and my brothers you are a foolish King, the devils wil say you hang Adam an slay all his Sons an not them, they came to take my Mother an sisters to protect them from you to populate the earth with gods as their are no Sons of my Father left on earth to pass on his holy seed to make holy people like us.

The commandant of soldiers next to Judah got afraid when the Sons of Adam shouted from their homes go away and leave us in peace, there was thunder and lightning.

Judah got angry because he did not want the gods to know Elijah brought him up from birth and taught him scriptures. The Elder said; Judah, the thunder and lightning is to warn you if you spill blood of my Father Sons, you will perish like god/cain who was born in sin like you. Judah spat on the face of the Elder, took out his sword and cut off one of his ear.

The Elder said, violence is in your nature, you cant stand to hear the truth. You are not of the pure race, you are a slave to do Satan, s evil work on earth, Satan is a rapist and murderer, it is he who strangled god /cain your father and took your Mother my Sister for himself in captivity while she was pregnant with you.

Judah spat in the Elder's face a second time, the soldiers held him down and began to kick him and began swearing fucking this an that who do you think you are, you insulted the king of gods.

The elder said; you bastards came to slay an spill blood of innocent Sons of my Father for doing no one harm, doing the same as god /cain who slay my brother Abel/Jesus because he was not righteous in My Father's Mothers flesh. And raped my sister to make a god like him with the wickedness of Satan.

THE TRUTH WILL SET ME FREE

Judah blocked his ear from this revelation, the Elder confirmed all what Elijah had told him in his youth about god/cain. Judah shouted at the Elder, shut up. The elder said the truth will set me an my Brothers Free to be with our Father who you do not know neither do you know god your/Cain your were father because you not born when he slay Abel and spill his blood.

Judah you hanged the body of my Father on the tree and want to slay my Brothers who did you no harm, if Elijah was your Father you would love me and my brothers, my Mothers an Sisters, but you are a god of god of Satan in conspiracy to make the Sons of my father extinct to hide the TRUTH and mislead gods to go astray with a false doctrin of devils, to hide your Identity, for gods to think you are self born and to live in Fear of devils, and to worship you as there mighty God to save them from devils after they are dead.

The Elder went on to say; god/cain your father was a lier, a conspirator in your Mother's captivity before Satan strangled him, he was possessed like you, their was no truth in him you are doing the same mistake in wanting to commit murder with hate for holy people, to please Devils. Judah, the devils are afraid of CHRIST and Elijah an gave you false hope after you die.

THE COMMANDER OF SOLDIERS

The commander of the soldiers said; King Judah, the law says any god who love CHRIST and Elijah to kill them, so pass judgment on this Elder and his Brothers who hate devils and you so we can retun to our nation.

THE HOUR HAS COME

Judah remembered what Elijah said, before they went their ways, I brought you up the good way, If you touch your mother or her people, ill abandon you. The commandant looked at Judah, he was in a trance hearing the voice of Satan in his head, telling him, kill Judah kill, Judah tried to lift up his sword to kill the Elder, the sword became heavy in his hand, he blocked his ears, hearing the voice of satan kill the Sons of Adam an leave the women to us.

Judah recomposed himself, got angry with hate and malice an said; Elder I herd all you had to say, is there any more of the truth of god / Cain my father you want to tell me before you are dead? The Elder said

I wish all gods will have Faith in Elijah to rest on the earth in peace. If any of my brothers or me die by you or your soldiers we will be with our Father in Heaven.

Judah said when you get their you will remember me for ever. Judah took his sword and pierced it in the heart of the Elder, the Elder fell, bleeding he looked upwards, and said, Elijah my Sprit is in your hands, then he collasped dead.

Immediately as the Elder died, the soldiers drew their swords and rushed inside the houses searcing for men old and young, even suckling baby boys and threw them outside, the soldiers outside with sharp cutlasses began to cut off the head of the the Sons of CHRIST / Adam and holding up their heads and throwing it away saying victory belong to the kings.

The women rushed outside their homes crying holding the dead body of their men and sons in their arms saying Lord have mercy they know not what they did, let all gods in the future know the truth, what Judah and his soldiers have done spillin the blood of your SONS your on earth.

The women took the blood gushing out of the neck of their loved ones an began washing their face and was beating there breast. Every where was dead bodies of men and their Sons from this bruitality an barbarity, Judah and his soldiers had no mercy. The heads of the men and their Sons scartered every where.

The women looked at Judah and his soldiers in shock and said blessed are the Sons that die like Adam, they shall see CHRIST. He will take vengence, and will do the same to you and your godly children on the days of Salvation and it will be justified to remove all gods from the earth. The soldiers laughed and said we dont care about salvation, then went in side the homes of the women an stole what they saw and went back outside and told the women to bury their dead men, and Sons.

Judah and his soldiers mounted their horses to leave. Eve went up and stood in front of the soldiers, looked at Judah. Judah said what do you want? Go and bury the the Sons you love.

Eve said; Judah today you have come against us. I am ashamed at your anger and taunts by your soldiers because you are not accepted, you came to take revenge on my Sons, Dont think paradise is lost today, but when Salvation begin every godly sprit from your seed shall perish after their body is dead. if they dont having Faith like you in Elijah.

It wll be justified when CHRIST take revenge for slayin suckling children by you and the battalion of soldiers you brought to make a mockery of me in this generation, the soldiers shall be witnesses to godly sprits for every generation on earth. When Christ Come on the days of salvation. He will do the same an cast out sprits of gods from his flesh, for judgment. Elijah promissed to return every godly sprit from you in the gate if you commit sin with your mother.

THE PAIN AND SORROW

Eve went on to say to Judah : The pain which I am suffering for my Sons, is the same every godly woman will feel when they bring a god in this world to live in fear of you, devils, and Death. The pain they will feel will be more unbearable when Christ cast them out, they will be without my flesh for sheding the blood of my Sons who was righteous in my flesh.

You have already condemned your self and all godly sprits born in your Mothers flesh for hanging the body Adam, your soldiers will be the witnesses for godly sprits in the final judgment in the time of salvation to tell them the Truth why they are not accepted like you

For not being righteous in the flesh of your Mother while she was pregnant with you, held in captivity by Satan to make gods in bondage Judah you shall have no peace. My Sons who you condemned are the blessed Sons of their Father from whose body you hanged on the tree. You will have no peace.

THE GATHERING OF THE DEAD BODIES OF THE SONS CHRIST/ADAM (Ro8.23/Mt24.31)

The women gathered the bodies of their Sons and their Brothers and counted them. It was 144000 and they buried the bodies, Took the heads and gathered them togethr an put them with the bodies.

THE FIRST RESURECTION OF THE SONS OF CHRIST/ADAM (1Cor15.12/Mk13.26.27}

The bodies of the Sons of CHRIST was put to rest, Their Sprits are immortal and in the Light, like CHRIST, and angels in heaven, they lay asleep in the graves. CHRIST on His throne in heaven sent Jesus to meet his brothers, Jesus waited for them in a pilar of cloud above the holy nation to show them the way to heaven. (Rev9.1)

Three days after while the Sprits of the Sons of CHRIST and Zion/Eve was asleep in the grave, the wind came and began to blow strongly, the leaves on the trees began to clap loudly, all the holy Women rushed out side their homes in the holy nation.

Elijah With the WORD said; Every Blessed Son of CHRIST that is asleep in the earth awake, leave your body an come forth from the grave and rise to the cloud to meet Jesus. The SPRITS from the Sons Of CHRIST and threir baby Christs came out from the graves and began walking on air, they looked same as their image when they lived in the flesh, The SPRITS of the Sons of CHRISTS began walking upward and waving their hands at the women while walking to the pillar of cloud over the nation.

When all the Sprits of CHRISTS got in the pilar of cloud with Jesus, Elijah commanded the winds to come unto the cloud and take Jesus and his Brothers to the throne to meet CHRIST their Father in heaven. (act17.24)

The wind came unto the cloud an it vanished taking the Sons of CHRIST to his throne in heaven to celebrate the victory over devils of Death on earth. Their was claping in heaven and joy on earth praising Elijah for resurecting the Sons of CHRIST from their sleep to be among Angels in Heaven with Everlasting life. (Deut1.10)

These were the SPRITS from the Seed of CHRIST with Zion /EVE born in the Kingdon in the begining they were persecuted and murdered by gods of the devils. The Sons of CHRIST shall see the final judgment on devils, Judah and godly sprits to Death,. be fore salvation in Kingdoms on earth begin (Rev 14.13:20. 6:Is61. 9:Mt5.3)

The women returned to their homes, feeling uncomfortable, sad, gloomy, knowing the devils are coming. Zion/Eve went looking for Elijah.

ELIJAH DECLARE THE PLAN TO ZION /EVE

Zion/Eve met Elijah, She was crying, Elijah asked what is the matter? She said Elijah you are the Only Son CHRIST created on earth with the WORD. I am in distress, all my Sons with Christ is extinct from the earth, how can my daughters populate holy people on earth if their are no Sons of CHRIST to pass on His seed to make immortal Sprits in our flesh? Elijah could you tell me what are your plans for me and my daughters? You are the only Son of CHRIST with the WORD I can turn too.

Elijah said; Eve, I declare to you which has not yet been done with the WORD with Me, to execute judgment on the devils on earth, making gods in your daughters flesh under oath. CHRIST will deside the time for Salvation to remove sprits of gods from Kingdoms from her flesh, and the godly sprits that prepare their body for Salvation and have faith, their godly sprits will rest in peace for their kingdom to be created by Christ.

Eve said; Elijah, When Christ come to create Sprits in Kingdoms for salvation will the sprits of gods in the kingdom care to know the Truth? Will they prepare their kingdom for salvation?

Elijah replied. The sprits of gods have a choice to have Faith to save them from Death while they live in the kingdom to rest in peace because they are not accepted by the ETERNAL SPRIT to live among angels in the heavens. Salvation will not begin until you are on the throne in heaven to see CHRIST cast out sprits of gods from your flesh and Tamah's for taking the kingdom by force.

CHRIST WILL MAKE WHAT IS IMPOSSIBLE WITH DEVILS POSIBLE THROUGHN ELIJAH

The devils have left the good life in heaven and come to earth to make godly sprits in your flesh with disease from Death, Satan and his devils has made much trouble for you Eve, first Satan raped you to make a god/cain. His god/cain raped your daughter to make a god like him, his son Judah hanged the body of CHRIST (Adam) and slay all your Sons without mercy with his battalion who are also witnesses for gods in later generations.

Elijah went on to say; Eve, Judah and his soldiers slay all your Sons and hanged the body of CHRIST, it opened the way for salvation to save your flesh from going to waste so CHRIST can create immortal SPRITS in the best of kindoms prepared for Salvation by the WORD to continue in their images to be productive making perfect Sprits to pass on the blessed holy sperm and egg of creation like angels in heaven.

THE TIME TO UNITE THE KINGDOM

Elijah explained the plan to Zion/Eve; When the time come to unite the kingdom with birth by the WORD and you will have a Blessed Son with the holy SEED to populate the earth with immortal SPRITS for you and CHRIST in kingdoms over the whole earth in righteousness not needing Salvation. If they die their Sprit will sleep and wait for CHRIST to take them to the heaven when he come to create Sprits in kingdoms for salvation.

Elijah explained the plan; He went onto say, Zion your flesh is your inheritance on earth, while sprts of gods live in your flesh the more seed of devils they pass, is the more kingdoms they make for CHRIST to create Holy Sprits in the best of kingdoms worthy to have a righteous Sprit to continue on earth to be productive making Sprits for the heavens with everlasting life.

The pain an grief you have suffeing for your Sons and CHRIST. When CHRIST return on the days of Salvation, He will create multitudes of Children in kingdoms for Salvation, regardless of skin colour or features on earth without suffering childbirth while you are in heaven as the Queen of all worlds. Elijah said Zion do you understand the plan I have for you and Tamah, an the choice the godly sprits have. Faith for peace or return to Death. Elijah said Satan has to repent for rape and holding Tamar in captivity he will be punished by Death.

All gods should have mercy on you for your distress and the suffering god/cain cause with deciet and conspiracy with satan. Judah and his battalion of soldiers has caused you an our people to suffer distress on earth. All gods are born in sin, the fault is with the devils of Death with disease poluting your flesh with death. Blessed are you Zion, your Spirit its immune to disease and so are all Sprits of Christ with everlasting Life.

Zion/Eve said; O Elijah you are my battle axe and weapons of war, Chase all the devils above the earth till they fall by the WORD.

Eliijah said; Zion I have declared to you judgment that has not yet been done by the WORD with me, the time will come when all devils on earth will be removed with righteous justice to execute judgment on all at the same time.

The sprits of gods will have until salvation to populate to make kingdoms for CHRIST to create Sprits so the earth can be populated with Righteous Sprits living in peace and harmony to be as it was in the begining without sprits of gods in your flesh world without end.

As they were about to part; Elijah said Zion, look upwards and see the the multitudes of stars, so will righteous Sprits populate the earth by CHRIST through the WORD with me. So be patient. When you return tell your daughters have no fear of devils, they can kill the body, but they can not kill their Sprit.

Zion/Eve said; O Elijah you have made this plan very clear, I will tell my daughters to be brave and have no fear of devils hold on to the Faith.

EVE RETURN TO HER DAUGHTERS

Eve returned to her daughters; Her daughters said Mother, what did Elijah say to you? Eve said, my children I am crushed by the trouble the devils will bring on us. When the hour come be strong and put your faith in Elijah and have no fear of devils. They cant kill your Sprit, Eve began to cry, their is nothing I can do.

Elijah said before we parted a great pleque will come upon you so be prepared for the worse and be brave an use restraint to enter heaven as inocents. He was sorry, and would not like us to be ignorant. The devils are planing to come after us take us in captivity so be prepared for the worst that can happen to you on earth.

JUDAH RETURN WITH HIS BATTALION

Judah returned with his battalion in the nation, and reported to Satan. O king all the Sons of Adam are now extinct from the earth only the women are left, none of the gods have interfered with them as you requested. Then left Satans, s office.

Immediately after Judah left, Satan called the chamberlain an told him to go and tell Queen Tamuze, Judah has slain all all her brothers only her Mother and sisters are left in the holy land and she must come to my bedchamber to make a petition to save them.

Tamuze came to his bedroom, she said, king what is your bribe this time, you decietfully ask me to come so you can satisfy your lust to save my Mother and sisters as if its a favour you are doing us.

I feel like a whore in this palace doing you a favour to make gods under oath, when I signed this oath I was in fear of you an the other devils. It was for you to leave my Father and Mother and all brothers and sisters I would have to live in peace you have not kept your word to leave my people in peace.

Satan you are a coward, Judah hanged my Father, s body on a tree, slew all my Brothers, and now you send for me to come to you to make a petition to save my mother an sisters from you. You sent Judah to kill my people for you because you are afraid of CHRIST.

Satan said; Tamuze it was in Judah, s heart to kill your people to live in my palace, he looked at your people as inferior to us devils, he hate your people because they depend on CHRIST and ELIJAH to save them from devils.

THE SEALED LETTER FOR gods
IN FUTURE GENERATIONS

Satan said; Tamuze, Judah is a now king of gods; It is he you should should fear his way is to use force to get what he want. I am worried the gods on earth will want to immitate him, worship him and make him think he is a mighty god because he is their king. Satan went on to say Tamuze if it will please thee, I will send Judah far away so he dont return to corrupt our gods with violence and war.

Tamuze said; I fear he will say its because of me you sent him far away, an devise some trickery to return to kill me. Please dont send him faraway. Satan said any thing to please you I will do? Tamuze said, put it in writing I asked you not to send Judah faraway an keep him as king of gods. And seal it with the ring on your finger, when you put it in writing You can satisfy your lust. Satan wrote her request with shaking hands and gave Tamuze the letter to keep for gods in future generations.

Satan said; now my queen undress, Tamuze said I have one more request, Satan said anything you say even half the earth, she said get rid of all the godly women in your harem, they have no respect for me when I go outside the palace they laugh at me.

They add to your sin for making them in my flesh give them all away as gifts to comandants of gods they are a burden to me, they have many faults and you spend to much time in the harem with these godly women, you cant satify these hungry bitches.

Satan said; They fight over me, you are never satisfied or like what I do, you say its disgusting and find fault with everything.

Tamuze said; You left the holy life above knowing what is good, but you behave like creatures on earth, you go on your knees and lick the godly women in the harem like a dog with lust.

THE FALSE KING

Judah began to boast among the gods, a god killed One holy Son in the begining but king Judah has slain thousands, to be your King, what the devils do I can do, I am a king with the kings on earth. Judah would kill any god who said anything against him, the gods began to live in fear of him.

THE CELEBRATION OF PARADISE LOST

Satan invited the kings and their godly queens, devils, and their godly women and commandannt and soldiers to celebrate Victory to populate the earth with gods, Judah did not come.

HOPE

There was abundance of wine a lot to eat, mucic and dancing every devil and god was merry giving praise to Satan for his vision to to be king of the world, Satan hoped Christ and Elijah had lost interest in Eve and her daughters on Earth and living the good life among angels in heaven.

The thaught of CHRIST and Elijah coming after him is always present and could not relax to celebrate victory with his guests he would scratch his head like a monkey, in this delemma to think straight. His sin, rapeing Eve to make a god brought back memories of his deciet, causeing him and other devils to be cast out of the heavens.

Now Eve has many daughters and his facing the same problem with rape, and the fear of CHRIST and Elijah coming to remove him and the other devils from the earth, make him sweat, hopeing this victory is permanent with no surprise attack on devils to end with Death.

Satan began to hate Tamuze, blameing her for his unhappiness, dictating what he should do with his godly women and calling him a coward, this sayings of Tamuze keep flashing in his head, you are a coward, it bothers him, an begin to swear in anger.

Saying I am surpose to be celebrating victory for the earth, drinking and eating with my guests and Im not happy, Tamuze delibrately stayed away, her absence, is messing up my mind. He called the chambelain and said go and tell Queen Tamuze to come to show the gods her beautiful face.

Tamuze was sorrowful and not in the mood for celebrating with devils and gods for the earth, her brothers was extinct from the earth and now uncertain future with her Mother and sisters. The fear of what Judah will do now, he is a king among devils with hate for her people.

The chamberlain came said; Queen Tamuze the king of nations want you to come and show your beautiful face to the gods.

Tamuze said; Go and tell your king when CHRIST and Elijah cast him in hell, there he will see beauty for killing pure holy people of the Eternal on earth. The chamberlain returned to tell Satan what Tamuze said.

This made Satan more angry, adding to his headach, he rushed to her room and said it is Judah who shed their blood, I am not your enemy, some times I feel to put my hands around your neck and break it like I did to cain.

Tamuze shouted, do it, break it now to take away my grief, or go away from me. Satan said; will you come out to meet the guest to celebrate the victory for the earth, or do I have to drag your ass out of the room, Tamuze cried you can do what you want as long as I dont see your face for another day to be free from this fucking oath.

Satan shouted you fucking bitch, when your sisters come in the palace I will take one of them to be my queen and you can kill yourself I will not care.

Tamuze loss her cool an said what was bothering her; I am glad its not you who had my verginity, god/cain whose neck you broke raped me to make a god to be wicked like you.

CONFRONTATION TORMANT HATE PAIN

Satan said; Ill break your neck like this fucker who took your verginity, if its the last thing I do on this earth, its because of raping your mother Im on earth and he has the done the same to you, now you are doing the same tormenting me like your mother when I was in heaven and was cast out for rape

Tamuze said; That is what you are a tormentor where ever you go. You are forceful you dont know what love is, you behave like the creatures on earth with lust, you feel you have power over women, you have abuse me an taken advantage of my kindness with this oat for peace. To keep away from my people.

You abuse the godly women in the harem, the stupid bitches fight over you, they make you feel important. You think my people are in ferior to devils and ignorant, we are creatures of the earth. When you can show me you can overpower CHRIST and Elijah, I will give you respect for the victory you are celebrating. You have made Judah kill for you so you and the other devils can go and rape my sisters. Satan you are a coward. A snake that run at the sound of an eagle.

Satan felt humilated by Tamuze and pushed her away from him with his head bursting with pain, and returned to his guests, all eyes was on him waiting for him to say something. But was in shock In great fear and have nothing to boast about. Tamuze called him a coward.

Satan began paceing up and down talking to him self. Hating Judah. The fucker did not turn up for the victory celebration, maybe some where drunk screwing and boasting he is the chosen god. Feeling his power is gone, CHRIST and Elijah is like a stumbling block, he cant aford to make a mistake. Tamuze is not afraid of me any more, she is dictating If I want respect I must overpower CHRIST and Elijah for the earth, her voice repeating coward show your power or no respect

Her voice is in his head coward, show your power its like a compulsive invisible force crying for her Father and brothers, the sound of crying is drilling in his head murderer, rapist, the scum on earth.

FALLING INLOVE IS RISKY

Satan began to feel he is in a trap saying falling inlove is risky its like going in quarantine ive become a slave to my lust. Hearing the crying of the mother of devils coming from far away, I warned you leave the woman and her daughter alone she is a trap for devils to fall, drilling noises in his head, all his guests are looking, he blocks his ears from far away crying of devils saying you are coming to join us with Death.

He is angry Tamuze dont care to see his face for another day, working himself to a frenzy, mixed with malice, jelousy, hate. The voice of the goddess crying in his head, she is your enemy kill her satan, she is only flesh and blood you cant satisfy this creature.

Satan realise he is a fool for faling inlove, her love for her people is more powerful than death of her body, she dont care if I kill her, she is not afraid anymore, Ive become transparent, she can see I am worthless, she is pressing me like a tempest that come and disappear, Ive become a slave to this bitch like a dog with lust and have to please her for peace in his head. This pain in his head was to much to handle.

Satan stoped the music and made a shot speach. He thanked every devil and god for the victory for the earth, then told the comanders and gods to go in his harem an take the godly women they liked as their gift and populate the earth with gods. Satan told the scribe to fetch Judah.

BABYLON

Judah arrived and Satan gave him a province, and proclaimed Judah as king of his province and all gods from his seed shall be his princes and prinsesses. Satan toasted with Judah and asked, what name shall you call the province. Judah said BABYLON.

TEMPTATION

After many months celebrations in the nations and everything carry on the same with gods working as slaves, building the nations, the Kings decided to meet in the synagogue to debate about Eve and her daughters.

A king said Satan; We have achieved victory on earth. I dont think CHRIST and Elijah will come to attack us, they are afraid of our gods or loss interest in the earth and enjoying themselves with the angels in the heaven and dont care about the holy people of Adam.

Another King said, Satan; My queen had a dream, she saw a god coming out of the body of a god, it came from no where, then he saw a woman, that made a god an the father of the god came from nowhere and then saw god the father and god the son began fighting for the woman. The mother of the first god began to cry an a holy One came he gave her a Son with the holy seed and he populated the earth with multitudes an she stop crying.

My queen began to cry in her dream, said the earth was full of light, their was no gods on earth, then she looked and began to see godly sprits decending to a Abys, then she saw Queen Tamuze with a holy ONE on earth and saw King Judah crying for Tamuze. The King said Satan my queen is crying and said if I go with you in the holy nation to capture the women I will not come back to her.

Another King said; satan, My queen had a dream, she saw the giant devils eating the remnants of the suckleing Sons of the Hebrew women and and they began to cry in pain.

Then she saw a god, a bright light came from its body an came to her face an said to my queen you will see what befalls the devils among this generation of gods. Then she saw big monsters opened their mouth an saw devils fallling one on top of the other in the mouth of the monsters. The king cotinued my queen is still trembleing with fright, she colapsed on the floor before I came to this meeting. The other kings began to look at Satan and was frightened.

Satan said; These these dreams are alot of deciet, all gods tell lies and full of jelousy an dream of what they cannot have an hope for a better life like the mother of devils. King devil could never satisy her. The godly women inherit this from her, that is why the world is divided because she wanted something better all the time. You are alowing your queens to frighten you so you dont come to capture the women to compete with them.

Satan went on to say to the Kings, I gave you the best of my princesses, I know them, from birth and they are full of tricks, they lie alot. You are devils, not gods, so stop telling your queens about when you were in heaven among beautful angels. You can not go back there neither any godly sprit from our seed is accepted by the ETERNAL.

If you gave your queens a good fuck before they go to sleep they would not dream, give them hard work or they will begin to curse you to leave the earth to go with gods.

SATAN DISCUSS HIS PLAN FOR THE EARTH WITH THE KINGS

Satan said to the kings, Ive given you kings the best of my godly daughters to be your queens to populate prince and princeeses on the earth to rule in the nations. We should concentrate on organizing our nations with laws and commandments according to the covenant with Death, so throughout all generations of gods live to pass on the seed of Death so the seed of gods dont diminish from populating godly sprits on earth.

Satan went on to say: Our gods dont know they are godly sprits while they live in the flesh of my queen, but when they are godly sprits without her flesh they will be like devils with spritual knowledge to fight against CHRIST and Elijah for the earth.

The godly sprits will be under oath, enter bodies and seduce sprits with lust to control governments and propergate religeon in different tongues to cause confusion to delay Salvation so the the whole earth will populate godly sprits without flesh of Adam and Eve.

After Satan explained his plan for the earth the kings said hail Cesar.

THE CAPTIVITY OF ALL THE WOMEN OF ADAM AN EVE

Satan told every devil that came to earth to report to him in the synagogue for a meeting. When all were gathered together. Satan said the time has come to capture all the women with Eve.

Some of you kings are backsliders an forget what we came to do on earth an expect me to go alone after the women, I am afraid. We all came to earth on a mission, and we are all in it together to capture all the women to propergate giants and gods.

Satan went on to say; Therefore, we should all bind ourselves to the oath according to the covernant with Death to pass on his seed to make sprits in their flesh so the seed of Death dont diminish, so sprits of gods cotinue to pass on his disease until all flesh is disease with Death.

By the time the earth is populated with our godly sprits, all flesh on earth will be diseased with death, there will be no flesh good enough for Christ and Elijah to use for Salvation that is where we will have victory when the earth will be inhabited with godly sprits from the seed of devils without flesh for Salvation.

After Satan discused his plan to capture the women to propergate godly sprits to take over the earth, he commanded the chief of the giant devils to come forward to sign the oath to bind himself to the oath, then the other giants, Naphilim, Raphaim, Emmin, Nuigual, Tiemel, Rami, Basha, Bati, Yetari, Baraguiv, Niplim, jamsi, Basham and Amaros. After the rest of the giants came foreward to sign the oath.

Satan said to the giants devils; you all were in reservations as a back up on this mission because I thaugt there would be trouble because the strength of CHRIST and Elijah has not been tested on earth. We dont know who they are, or have seen them, all we know if we made gods they will come against us. We have made many gods through my Queen and they have have not come to earth. Your time has come to implant the power of your seed in the holy women to make giants sprits to populate your kind on earth.

Satan said to the giants; When we go to the holy nation fuck many women to make giants an slay every sucklng male so the holy seed of Adam perish and giants sprits populate and rule over gods with your strength.

The chief of the eunuchs came forward with the eunuchs; Satan said to them, your work will be desided after we capture the women.

Satan striped the ten Kings of their crowns and made them commanders of 20 devils each. All the devils that came to earth signed the oath. Then he said to them all, I know the price of temptation is a reason to justify righteousness to eliminate us from the earth with no peace.

Therefore let no suckling male live to decive your giants. All the devils prepared their horses for the long journey. The gods in their nations came to wish the devils good luck. The scribe took count to make sure no devil was missing. The devils kissed their godly women and mounted their horses, Judah was with them.

Satan saw Tamuze standind by the gate outside the palace, he rode up to her and said my queen what is your request before I go and gather your people, it be granted thee? Make your request now before I leave you and it shall be given thee even half the earth.

Tamuze answered all flesh of gods on earth is my inheritance, If you want respect dont let Judah go with you let him stay while you are gone, I cant endure to think you are taking Judah with you to kill all my people to perish from the earth

Satan said Tamuze this mission is only for devils I'll let Judah stay in the castle to guard you so you dont kill your self while Im away.

Tamuze said; you live me with a murderer to guard me. How long are you going to be away? Satan looked at her with hate knowing if he did not go without judah Tamuze would call him a coward.

THE DEVILS RIDE OUT TO CAPTURE EVE AND HER DAUGHTERS

The devils rode out from the nation on horseback for the long journey to the holy nationto capture Eve and her daughters.

The women could here the noise of galloping horses coming closer and closer to their nation. When the devils arrived they surrounded the nation, Satan commanded the women to come outside their homes.

Eve came outside and said; What is it you want? I have nothing belonging to devils, you come shouting for me and daughters to come outside our homes, you are tresspassing will you leave in peace.

Satan said; Eve its because of you we are cast out of heaven to earth to be among creatures like you, for making one god with you! is my Sin. Now you have a multitude of blessed women in the nation to pick and choose, so tell the women in the nation to come outside to meet me and the rest of the devils to commit adultry. Adam and your Sons are not here to help you.

Eve said; Satan, as you can see we dont live in wall cities if you or any devil touch me or any women here, Elijah will come after you.

Satan said; Elijah will not come to earth to save you and your blessed women; He has lost interest in your people on earth. That is why Ive come with the other devils to take you back to our nation to make gods for us because Judah killed all your men.

CONFRONTATION

Eve said; Satan, you stole my daughter, and hold her in coptivity to make gods in her flesh, every god that is born shall fall on your head. You had Judah to hang Adam who is better than you, all of you are degenerates and a bunch of cowards who come to attack blessed women of the Eternal when their holy men are dead.

Satan said; Eve, your god (cain) with me wanted to make a name for himself to be the first to F . . . k Tamah to make a god like himself to pass on my seed. I told Judah not to kill you and the women, so come back with us to our nation.

Eve said to do what? No god can go to heaven where you came from, nor will any god be on earth when CHRIST come to establish kingdoms from my flesh Elijah will prepare for Salvation, you are a liar and a thief so leave in peace Satan, and all the devils that came with you came with deciet to repeat what you did in the garden of Eden to rape me and my blessed women.

Satan said; Eve, believe me this time, Ive information Elijah and Christ is not coming to earth to save your daughters, He did not come to save Adam from Judah, why do you think he will come to save you and your daughters and Tamah in my palace burdened with Sin?

So tell the women to come out to meet devils who came from a long journey to meet them an take them to their nations flowing with milk an honey and it will go well with them when they make gods for them, Eve, there are no moor Sons of Adam to give them holy children to populate on earth. It seem good to come with us to populate the earth with gods from our seed to live under the covenant of Death.

Eve said; I am of creation, I am not from Death you are from the seed of Death. My daughters are freeborn, same as me in the Flesh and not gods from the seed of devils who are strangers on earth with lust to sin in holy flesh, forbiddon to strangers on earth. CHRIST and Elijah will not like us making gods for devils to end with Death.

In regards to god (cain) whose neck you broke, Elijah raised his son from the bush who is now your chief Prophet with commandments and laws and king of gods, you are decieved by him and if you dont leave in peace with all your devils, he will rule your palace. He did not love his neighbour, but came here like you with hate, malice, jelousy to spill blood of Adam. Elijah did not accept him, because he is a god born in Sin and had no Faith for peace. This apply to every god born in holy flesh who has no Faith will recieve a severe sentence for hanging Adam. Eve went on to say; Satan you and your devils come here like thieves, tresspassers to take advantage of holy women without their men leave in peace.

Satan; Eve said, Ive asked you to leave in peace, your presence here is threatening our peace we want to grieve our men you sent Judah to slay if you or any devil rape any woman in this holy land it will be the last day for every devil upon the face of the earth, we are always prepared to die, we are not afraid of devils, I can assure every one of you. Elijah will chase you out of the earth with pleasure. This speach by Eve put fright in Satan he did not expect her to talk to him this way with knowledge.

Satan said; Eve, where is Elijah? Tell him to come and I will belive you? Eve answered, He is slipery like soap. He appears and disappears and never stay in one place, He has eyes that can see what you dont see, and ears that can hear that you cant hear, and can speak the word that can be heard from earth to heaven an from earth to the roof of heaven. If I open my mouth Elijah will come to remove you and every devil above the earth.

Eve went on to say, I made a god for you because you raped me, you and devils were cast out of heaven for rape, for makeing a god in sin The same will happen to you and every devil if any devil commit rape in this holy land. Every one of you will be chased out from the face of the earth an fall never to return above the earth for ever.

Satan said; Eve, Elijah has told you many lies, unless I see Elijah with my two eyes I will not belive He and CHRIST exist, so tell the women to come outside, if Christ is in heaven he will see devils rape holy women to populate the earth.

REPENT SATAN

Eve said Satan you are an idiot and a coward, you better repent for raping me, and stealing my daughter an holding her in your palace in bondage.(Thou shall not steal). you have made gods with her under oath. Repent and set her free from your palace. Elijah will have no mercy on you. He can give her children of creation that will be accepted in heaven. That is imposible with you but is posible with Elijah through Christ.

FEAR AND ANGER

Satan got angry; said, who you think you are, no creature on earth can have heavenly exsistence like holy angels in heaven, a devil near by said; Satan this creature is insulting you and want you to repent to give you mercy, tell her devils have no mercy, because of her The Eternal had no mercy on us, She called you an idiot to come to earth to rape her to make a useless god that had no power.

Eve said; Satan, dont you see your situation on earth is hopeless, you will always live in fear if you tresspass in forbiddon flesh the Eternl Created. For one Sin, you are all cast out of heaven, and today all of you are about to be removed from the earth if any rape is commited with blessed women in this nation. Adam lived 950 years on earth among creatures in peace an harmony and taught his people scriptures, you think we are ignorant. Elijah will do righteous justice for us if you or any devil have sex with holy women this day. Every devil will be punished and returned to Death for ever. Satan; Eve said, this is the ultimatum leave the earth in peace an return to where you came from.

Satan felt humiliated, Eve made him feel like the scum on earth, commanding him to Repent for raping her and stealing her daughter, and holding Tamah in captivity his head is spining in pain, the voice of Tamuze calling him, coward, Eve calling him coward and telling him Judah is about to take over his palace, Repent, or face judgment, the eyes of all devils are on him. He is flabbergasted, he dont realize its Zion speaking through the mouth of Eve, nor can any devil comprehend all the blessed women are immortal Sprits in the light in their image in the flesh, thinking they are just flesh and blood like creatures.

Zion (Eve) is pressing him, Repent coward, one word from my mouth an you and all devils will be flying like a kite to hades. He thinks Eve is bluffing, No devil can see Immortal Sprits in the flesh. Satan and the other devils have not experienced Judgment by Elijah. Or know He is created with the WORD By CHRIST when He was in the body of Adam to be the judge of the whole earth and Saviour of Sprits in the Light and establish Kingdoms for Salvation.

Satan immagin all eyes in heaven is watching him conered by a creature on earth, no place to hide. Eve is showing him She is not afraid, saying, its better to die like Adam and live like CHRIST, we are all ready to die so we dont see your face another minute, Elijah will be the Judge. Repent, murderer, sex with devils is punisable by Elijah.

The devils said Satan she is talking in parables we dont understand the scripture of this creature, our covenant is with Death and by this covenant she and all the blessed women of Adam ought to die like Him.

ZION (EVE) WARN SATAN gods WILL BE KINGDOM MAKERS FOR SALVATION

Eve said; Satan if you or any devil commmit Rape with blessed women shall perish and leave your gods to make kingdons for salvation for their peace if they have Faith. Repent for raping me and stealing my daughter.

Satan said fuck you Eve, I will not Repent, we will fuck the holy women and full their stomach with drunks like Judah and all kind of sinners in holy flesh with diseased from Death until all flesh disappear on earth like a mist that is here today gone tomorrow forever. Eve I will not repent to you or CHRIST or Elijah. I am in the world before you and them. I am a king, Now you come and bow to me before all devils, Ive conquerd the earth for gods in all generations to inherit

Eve said; I will not bow to an idiot, you have a choice to repent but if you choose to disobey you will be condemning yourself to face Death for ever for rape and stealing my daughter. This apply to every devil who commit rape, will also condemnd themselves with you. And so is every god who has no Faith in Elijah for Peace. She said I shall not speak to you for ever. Eve walked away and went inside her home.

RAPE

The devils began to look at Satan, stunned by Eve, s reaction showing no fear and prepared to die than respond, he felt like a begger, Eve want repentance for raping her doing him no favour. His plan has many holes, all he has left is hope or fall in a trap. Satan began to hear the goddess crying in his head, I warned you leave the woman an her daughter alone. They are a trap for all devils to fall, Tamuze screaming at him kill me do me a favour, now she is with Judah, Eve calling him an idiot, feeling like a rat that is connered, his head is bursting with pain and disappointment, drilling noises in his head, he could not take the preasure, to much pain, to much ambition to rule the world as king devil. to much lust for power, to much desire to rule and control others to bring the world back to darkness, comming against Christ and Elijah as a stumbleing block with Fear of falling and not seeing Tamuze again in the palace to face Death.

To be where no devil has been in the lower rigeon of the earth is fear of Elijah and CHRIST is like facing Death if he fail with his plan. The eyes of every devil is on him. He said to hell, put down his thumb and all the devils rushed in inside the houses and began to rape the women.

The giant devils began to eat the suckling baby boys, blood coming out of their mouth, going from house to house raping the women and eating their baby boys, the giant devils would hold the women in one hand and ravish them with intense passion, the women would cry in pain and faint and would be cast outside their homes when they defile them, they would go to another, would curse them fucking this and that whore and eat their crying baby boys then after they fuck them to make them pregnant with giant gods then they would throw the women outside their homes, when they satisfied their lust and had enough.

THE HOLY LAND BECAME A LAND WITH MURDERERS AND RAPISTS SPILLING BLOOD

The devils chained the women one to another and brought them out of the nation, and set their houses on fire. The devils mounted their horses, the women followed them by foot. Some cried for rest. They were floged with rods to move on, they were thirsty on this journey stagering and falling on top each other and weak they held on to their faith in their Saviour Elijah. Finaly the devils got thirsty and left the women, and went to the lake to drink water an to give their horses water.

Eve fell upon her knee and spread out her hands and said Elijah. I am ashamed to even lift up my face to thee. The devils have raped my daughters and burnt all our homes to ashes and hold us in captivity in chains in this miserable place.

JUSTICE AND JUDGMENT
JOB36.17/PS9.16/ps103.6

Eve said; Elijah, my flesh has become unclean with the abomination of devils, they have poluted the flesh of my daughters with the disease of Death to prevent Salvation, Elijah I want Justice. Satan raped me to make god (cain), and stole my daughter Tamah and hold her in captivity, all the devils came to our nation, raped my daughters and eat their baby boys, set fire to our houses, and have us in chains in captivity in this miserable place as you can see shivering from this abuse by all devils on earth.

Elijah; Im oppressed by the tyranny of Satan and all the devils on earth, I appeal to you to minister righteous justice for all the suffering the devils have afflicted unto your people on earth, so we are not humilated anymore by devils on earth. Elijah pass righteous judgment on all devils on earth today for their brutality, murder, rape and theft of my daughter to make gods in the flesh of CHRIST an ZION without our consent.

ELIJAH EXECUTE JUDGMENT FOR ZION/EVE
By TORNDO PS>83.13 IS33.5.29.5)

Elijah spoke in the ears of Eve; Zion Tell the women to stick close together to see judgment on all devils on earth as requested. Elijah commanded mist to come, it came an covered where the women were.

The devils began to mount their horses, lightning began to zig zag and loud thunder came over where the devils were and it frightened the horses, the devils fell off the back of the horses Then an earthquake came and the horses took off, the devils began to chase after the horses, Elijah commanded the tornado to come, an it came in a wirlwind in devouring fire and it hoovered all the devils in the wirlwind and carried them all away.

The tornado droped the devils, and they began to fall one on top the other in the mouth of sea monsters, then the monsters journeyed to the deep in hades. When the sea monsters got to the gate of hades it opened automatically and the monsters spat out the devils inside the gate, and it was locked automaticaly in hades, their the devils will wait until final judgment before salvation begin on kingdoms and final Judgment on gods on earth

Satan and the devils were astonished to see the goddess of the ancient world of darkness as the receptioness with a book in hades to take count of the godly sprits cast out of the earth from seed of satan and other devils passing the seed of Death to make gods in the flesh of CHRIST an ZION.

The goddess took count of how many devils that came from from the ancient world to the earth. She said; Satan I told you to leave the woman (Eve) alone, you would be back, she put all the devils in the chambers in hades and kicked the switch and they fell to the lower rigion of hades. The fire in the earth was ignighted for the devils to wait for godly sprits CHRIST will cast out from the flesh of Zion (Eve) and all His daughters, on the days of Salvation to Create immortal Sprits to unite the Kingdoms worthy of Salvation for it to be as it was in the begining with no gods in holy flesh of creation to live in peace and harmony on earth until their Sprits resurrect to be with angels in heaven for ever.

Zion (Eve) said; Elijah, you have saved us with Tornado and righteous judgment. The devils did not expect swift judgment by the WORD with you in this miserable place. Elijah said hold on to your faith.

JUDGMENT (Ps9/12-16) ON ALL ANCIENT DEVILS THE WARNING BY ELIJAH IN SIN MY MOTHER CONCIEVED ME (PS51.5)

Judah was in the palace meditating, introspective of his youth. Elijah had told him, Im not your father dont go and tell any one Im your father, You have no Faith so I can create a Sprit in your body to be my Son for you to rest in peace. Elijah had told him Tamuze was his mother an she was held in captivty by devils, if he had faith in Him he would go and save his mother an if he needed help call Him. He did not.

Elijah warned him if you fornicate with your mother ill abandon you and all sprits fron your seed you will recieve at the gate. Your mother, s flesh is her inheritance to create Sprits in Kingdom for Salvation.

KING JUDAH (Ps 147.1-5/Gen11.1-4)

King Judah was meditating on setting up his province Satan had given him to rule gods as their king, he was ignorant of Death. Elijah had told him the truth about his birth an told him all what he shouldnt do. He had a choice to follow the way Elijah had taught him.

QUEEN TAMUZE

For the first time Tamuze had the oppertunity to be in the palace with Judah alone, she began to feel restless. She anticipated Judah would come after her, she was puzzled he kept away. She did, nt know Judah was her first god with cain she had given birth in the bush and had covered him in straw to prevent Satan from eating him when she gave birth to him.

Tamuze had Faith in Elijah she had not seen to save him from Satan who had warned her if its is male god ill eat him from birth, and if its a female god ill accept to make gods with devils.

Tamuze asked the two servants to massage her, thinking it would relax her from this restlessness and fear of Judah but the massaging oil had a stimulating effect on her, She became curious and wanted to know why Judah killed her Father and and all Brothers. She told the servants to go and tell Judah she wanted to speak with him. She remained naked on the couch.

The servants went to Judah and said King Judah Queen Tamuze desire your company. Judah followed the servants to the Queens, s room, the servants closed the door behind them and kept watch, not knowing of the judgment on all devils.

THE NACKEDNESS OF YOUR MOTHER
(Lev 18.7/Deut27.23

Judah stood by the door with his hands folded looking at his mother, s nakedness and well shaped body. Tamuze looked at him closely and had a sensation in her womb, remembering the feeling of her first god moving inside her while pregnant in the dungeon in captivity by Satan.

She was in a trance thinking back and now this god in her bedroom much feared for his cruelity, she could, nt understand why she was feeling this way. Satan had defiled her with lust for her flesh with sexual passion of all sorts with force and hate for who is holy.

(Gen2.25-14) BONE OF MY BONE
FLESH OF MY FLESH

Tamuze began thinking here I am with this murderer in my bedroom. Instead he do like Satan an F . . . k me by force, he is only looking at my nakedness.

(Deut27.23) Cursed is the son of god who lieth with his mother in bondage to devils and betroth her in captivty under the law of devils (Deut29.19-22:Deut27.23).

Judah said, you called for me, what do you want? Tamah tempted him and opened her legs an said judah you know what I want, Judah stood by the door looking at her naked remembering the words of Elijah; he know tamuze is his mother, but she dont know Judah is her first god.

Tamuze was amaized at Judah standing with his hands folded an standing, making no atempt to molest her, She got up from the couch an went on her knee on the carpet and began crawling slowly towards him, She said; Judah can I touch you? Ive wanted to do this since the first time you came to the palace, Judah said nothing. She put her hands around his legs. (Col2.21)

Judah felt a rush of blood all over his body, she felt the same feeling of close attachment which had disappeared suddenly when she gave birth to her first god in the bush, the relief of giving birth in fear of Satan eating him from birth. Tamuze kept holding on to his legs an began crying.

Judah is tempted, the warning of Elijah instilled in him dont fonicate with your mother, you can fonicate with godly women, he can not tell tell Tamuze to stop crying, he is her first god, he is tempted to F . . . k his mother.

Tamuze said; you are the only one between me an Elijah in my room, why are you standing their like a hungry god lusting for flesh? Don't you have feelings? F . . . k me or kill me.

ABOMINATION 1COR 7.1/ PS91.1-8

Judah picked up his mother in his arms, she held on to him, the smell of musk and goat was on him like Cain and she began to remember that smell on Cain while he was raping her saying flesh of my mothers flesh while raping her. Judah began to F . . . k like his father in abomination an she passed out, an slept in his arms.

DREAM OF TAMUZE

Tamuse dreamed all her people was gathersd together in a place and judjment had been passed on devils and she saw the devils decending to the deep and in chambers crying, and saw Judah bound in a chamber in snow and multitudes of gods coming out from there body and by a tempest and began to fall one on top the other, and the dream disappeared.

FEAR IN THE NATIONS (Rev17.5-16/Mt19.24-24)

Elijah commanded fire balls to fall on the houses in the nations followed by lightning an thunder houses began to be on fire the gods began to be afraid runing here and there trying to put out the fire saying its the end of the world, crying for the devils to come back from the holy land, rain began to fall, lightning and thunder and no sunshine in the nations in the day, the moon blood red in the night.

The princes from the other nations came to the palace of satan and ask to see Judah, The servants went to tell Judah the princes wanted to see him, he was with Tamuze he came out from her room, asked what do you want? One princes said, Judah since the devils left there is much disturbance on earth, you are the only king left, do you know why?

Another prince said; Judah my queen mother cant stop crying for our king since he left us, she said something has happened to him and the other devils. Judah come with us to show us the way to the holy nation to look for the devils. Judah excused himself and went to the bedroom told Tamuze he was going to look for the devils, she said they will not return I saw them fall and going in the deep in a dream. He kiss her and left to join the princes to look for the devils.

REVELATION 17/18.7 I SIT AS QEEN
I AM NO WIDOW

When they got to the place the devils had called armageddon, the women saw judah and other riders coming towards them, they cried Judah is coming to kill us, Eve said have faith in Elijah.

Judah and the princes came to where all the women were gathered, they screamed at Judah the devils are gone; Judah asked in what direction did they go? they did not answer, one of the princes said, my queen mother is crying for our king, where did the devils go? Eve said to the prince if you want to know, all tthe devils have gone to hades, they are waiting for you their.

Another prince asked where is the road to hades so we can ride to meet them? Eve said, Judah knows, who was the first to go to hades for rape, but you have to be dead to go their by a wirlwind to meet the devils in hades.

Another prince asked, what do a wirlwind do if am dead, Eve said ask Judah he will tell you, but drink alot of water first before you go on the journey, the devils were thirsty and drank alot of water by the lake and they were taken away by a Tornado swiftly. So tell your mother all the devils was removed from the earth for violence and rape

The princes looked at Judah for an answer, the women were looking at Judah to see what he would do, they said to the princes he hanged my Father and slay all our brothers he is next King to join the devils.

ELIJAH AND JUDAH

Judah saw a man standing under a tree at a distance and percieved it was Elijah. Judah rode up to Elijah. Elijah looked at him, Judah said what are you doing under this tree?

Elijah said do you want bread to fall from the sky to eat with the princes of devils or wine to celebrate the havest the devils left behind to share with the princes of devils.

Judah said I will not take a shoelace from thee or any women in this place, lest you say you have saved me to show me your power, so was his arogance, hate for holy people.

Elijah said if I were hungry I would not tell thee, thou has cast my Word behind thee when thou sawest your mother, you had lust to fornicate with her instead of saving her from devils, You hanged her Father an slay all the brothers of your mother to be a king, these things you have done.

Elijah went on to say, you thought I was a god like you when I brought you up, an hated me for telling you the Truth. I am not god your father and was the first in Salvation in his dead body, if you had Faith an offered your body for salvation I would have had it created with a Son to be like me in creation and your godly sprit yould have rest. You did not belive or had faith, that was your choice to rest in peace or fall like devils. You are commiting abomination with your mother doing the same as god your father and the devils.

I could tear you appart for having no faith, an for all the wickedness you have done, and send you to join the devils for you to see if they can do anything for you. You have made me ashame, I brought you up the good way, but you have allowed the devils to decieve you by making you their prophet to teach gods to live by the covennant with Death. You have become an alian unto your Mothers people.

ELIJAH WARN JUDAH

Elijah said, Judah if you fornicate with any of the women to multiply gods with your accursed seed of god you father, there godly sprits shall go inside the gate of hades to join god your father with the devils. Their kingdoms shall be the blessings on earth and not your godly sprits from the the accursed seed of satan and the devils I removed from the earth for rape and violence.

Now that you are a Prophet with the laws of devils and king of gods, make this be known to gods before they pass on the seed of devils to make godly sprits to live unto the covernant with Death while they live in your mother's flesh.

Judah asked Elijah how did you removed the devils from the earth? Elijah replied by a tornado for commiting rape with the blessed women and kidnaping your mother to make gods in her flesh and making you slay holy Sons of the earth. Judah I have restrained from all sorts to kill you before Christ come. But Christ said vengence belong to him for hanging his body on a tree and slaying all his Sons. You have condemned your self for having no Faith for Peace.

Judah was afraid and bowed his head in shame, and relised Elijah had pity and gave him more time on earth to do good for the gods.

Elijah said I will chastise thee with much punishment if you harm or do wickedness to your mothers Mother and her sisters so you may know the WORD with me do Righteous Justice and righteous Judgment on all gods on the face of the earth from now on.

THE SECRET KING JUDAH KEPT TO HIMSELF. Dan2/47

The princes came to Judah and asked who is this old god? Judah kept the secret of Elijah and Christ to himself to make gods think he is self created an all on earth must call him the mighty God the chosen god of the whole earth, the only king of kings left to rule all on earth.

JUDAH and EVE

Judah asked Eve; Did Elijah save all your daughters from Satan and the other devils? Eve asked what meanest thou to ask if Elijah saved all my daughters, the devils raped my daughters and brought us in this dreadful wilderness shivering with grief, they defiled them and burnt all our houses.

Now we are before a murderer and princes of devils saying their godly queen mothers are crying for rapist devils, yes Elijah removed the devils from the earth with swift judgment for his blessed people on earth.

Judah got the princes to one side and began to debate, one prince said there are so many holy women what can we do with so many that look like queen Tamuze. Judah said if we leave them here, we will all perish like the devils. I suggest one of you ride back to the nation an see the commandant of my battalion and tell him to come with many horses and carts he can find in the nations to bring the women in the nations, meanwhile the women will follow after us till you return.

Judah and the princes divided the women between themselves to live in the harems of their palace and set the godly women free. Haveing agreed what they are going to do they unchained the women and they began to follow Judah and the princes on the journey towards the nations, some women fell and died of exhaustion, some died of thirst when the battalion of soldiers arrived some went on horse back others in carts, when they finaly got to the nations, gods were stareing at them an calling them names

Hebrews, Hebrews, witches because of you the devils have gone away, as they passed they spat, dont bring them here to do socery on gods to leave the nations, as they passed they threw stones at them shouting go away. The prices took the women to their palaces to live in their harems, It was easy for Judah to put the women in the houses of the godly women Satan had given to his soldiers as a gift to please Tamuze.

THE TRUTH WILL SET YOU FREE / Jn843-44

Judah went inside the palace an saw Tamuze and told her Satan and all the devils have perished from the the face of the earth by Elijah. Tamuze began to dance an sing I am no widow or queen of devils, I am free today from this oath. Now Satan shall cry for taking me in captivty to make gods to marry in my flesh. Judah let us give praise to Elijah for righteous Judgment on all the devils for raping my Mother to make a murderer and conspirator with Satan to hold me captive all these years. I am free.

Tamuze began to sing My Father told me before satan held me in captivty. Elijah will save me, I have faith one day ill see my first god I ask Elijah to save from satan.

Judah could not humble himself to tell Tamuze that he was her first god Elijah found in the bush and brought him up as his begoten god,

Elijah called him Ammon before Satan called him Judah. In fear Eve would tell Tamuze that he was her first god with cain, Judah gave a guard strict orders, no woman in the harem is allowed to come inside the palace to see queen Tamuze or even talk to her.

TAMUZE ASK JUDAH TO REJOICE WITH HER FOR BEING FREE FROM THE OATH Re12.1.12

Tamuze said, Judah rejoice with me, all the devils are gone to the bottom of the sea, Elijah has passed judgment on all of them for rape and decieving you. I had to endure all this abuse for peace to keep the devils away from my Father an Mother and my people. Now you are a king in the eyes of Elijah so dont be a foolish king like the kings of devils, ill sit as a Queen of Peace in this palace in the eyes of Elijah, any god that disturb my peace Elijah will send them in captivity to join the devils.

Judah said my plan is to rule the whole earth after I am dead with godly sprits to fight with me against Elijah for the earth. To make war on all till their is no flesh left from you or your mother and sisters for salvation godly sprits without your flesh is my gain to be king of all sprits from your blessed flesh.

Tamuze took pity on him an said; Judah you can live in the palace in peace till you build your palace in Babylon, take this oppertunity to do good for gods now while you are alive, what good will it do if you gain all godly sprits from the seed of devils after they live the flesh of my Father and Mother. When CHRIST come on earth is for salvation for kingdoms of gods, and when He cast out sprits from my flesh, Elijah will only save godly sprits who has faith in him to rest in peace according to the scriptures My Father taught me.(Mt16.23-28)

Judah said, Im not accepted in heaven even if I do good on earth, because I am a god, Elijah ofered me peace for my sprit to sleep in peace for ever, I had no faith in his peace. It is through my wickedness

I am a king of gods. Tamuze he said: Im not like you who have faith in Elijah to save you to live forever. I am a king of kings. A mighty god.

Tamuze said; Judah you live in hope you will be king of the sprits of gods from my flesh, god Cain my brother in my mothers flesh conspired with satan before he raped me to make a wicked god like him to be prince of the earth and he ended in hades. If you loose the battle for the earth you will end in hades an the devils will laugh at you, if you go through this plan to fight against Elijah.

Think Judah, if Elijah removed the devils from the earth for rape and cruelty to my people, and you have godly sprits declare war to distroy everybody with the flesh of my Father and Mother. Elijah will pass judgment on multitudes of godly sprits and it will be justified to send them in captivity to face Death for ever.

Judah if you taught gods to have faith in Elijah they could have a choice to have Faith to rest in peace, rather suffer in fire for ever with devils and Death. That is why Elijah offered you peace to teach gods to have Faith in Him as their saviour. Tamuze went on to say, Judah this plan only Death will gain all godly sprits through ignorance of truth.

Elijah is for peace, what make you think godly sprits will fight for the earth with you? They are not honest they might fight against you if you decieve them. And they get to know your wickedness. All flesh of gods is my inheritance on earth so for get this plan you will make Elijah angry with you. My Father told me to have Faith in Elijah. Accept the way you were born, while you are king and have faith for peace.

CURSED IS HE WHO LIETH WITH HIS MOTHER
(Deut.27.23)

What Tamuze said to him went in one ear an out of the other, Judah held Tamuze in his arms and carried her to bed, he said you are my queen, Tamuze said you are forceing youself on me dont, stop what you are doing you are a god, it is forbiden, I am free from the oath dont add to my sin you will make Elijah angry with me. You hanged my Father and slay all my brothers I cant, stop it, its rape.

Judah inflamed with lust, he kissed her, she slaped his face, he grined, I am your king bone of your bone as long as I am in your flesh ill fuck you until I depart from it. Tamuze began to cry, stop forcing yourself you are commiting rape, its forbiden if I concive a god for you it will be born in sin.

The godly queens came to see Judah, the servants knocked on the bedroom door, Tamuze asked what you want? They said the queens of the nations want to see King Judah, Tamuze said why dont you make one of them your queen an leave.

Judah came out from the room angry, one of the queens rushed an held on to him an began to cry, O king will the devils come back? Life is unbearable without my king, I cant sleep and have bad dreams since he left. Judah said the devils will not be coming back for ever, I am the the king of of the whole earth. Tamuze is now my queen, I set her free from the oath by my power, an is my queen according to the law. The queens returned returned to their nations and made their princes their kings.

KING JUDAH OF BABYLON (Jn.10.34)

Judah concentrated in building his palace in Babylon for he and Tamuze, he boasted he is the chosen god with knowledge of arts and craft and scripture of ancient civilization to build Babylon to be the greatest nation on earth

He compared himself to be more powerful than the Lord of Storm and winds, earth quakes, lightning and thunder. The gods worshiped him as their Mighty God who removed the devils from the earth.

THE BEGINING OF MANKIND (Gen1.12)

The queens began to get jelous of their kings paying much attention to the holy women in captivity, with much jelousy an aguements they began to sell some of the pregnant women to rullers of gods in their nation to propergate and sell their children.

THE MARRIAGE IN FLESH (JN3.3-6)

Judah said; Tamuze, Satan is not returning, I am king of Babylon you are free from the oath, according to the law I am going to marry you in the flesh to make children to look different from gods you made with satan.

Tamuze said, what will you call them? Judah said ill call them Isralites. Maybe Elijah will accept them to go to heaven. There is no one like your brothers left on earth with pure seed to make your kind of people, after your sisters give birth to gods, ill make children with your sisters and will mingle them with your children to populate my creation with new features.

Tamuze said, you rape me to make me pregnant in the palace of satan to add to my sin and want to make my sisters pregnant for you to mix and mingle features to look like people you killed to provoke Elijah to make him angry with me.

VIOLENCE ANGER CURSEING AND HATE

Judah got angry, he hit her with the rod he hit the horse Adam sat when he hanged him and said. I call this rod nimrod and it will do the same to you if you dont worship me as your king. From now on you will no more be called queen Tamuze but Queen of Babylon with your king to rule your mother and sisters and all on earth.

Like a tyrant and angry with nimrod in his hand he said, now kneel and worship your king Queen of Babylon, she began to cry, have mercy on me you are doing this to provoke Elijah. He slaped her she began to tremble an was in shock. He began curse f . . . . get up and worship your king.

Tamuze cried you are a devil, you are no damn good, fucking and curseing me with your tongue you are a distroyer of holy people Elijah will cast your ass out of this palace (1Pet.4.12.16:Ps.107.1-9 Rev13.5-8).

The devils will laugh at you, for having no Faith for peace by Elijah. I am pregnant with your israelite, is this the way you treat me with no loving kindness? You make me ashame to bring another like you from my flesh in sin, Instead of leting me enjoy my freedom in peace you keep me in captivity like satan to make isrelites to live under the law, you are disgusting.

SILENT IN SUBMISSION
(1Tim1.7-8/iTim2.8-11/1Cor.14-34-36)

Judah felt humiliated by Tamuze an held her neck and said ill kill you. No one can satisfy you, you are like whores in Babylon who can never have enough, every time you mention Elijah you will taste nimrod to learn to be silent an submit to your king, and this goes for your mother and sisters in the harem quarters.

Tamuze shouted you bastard, you want to take over the palace of satan with your laws and rules, kill me with this Israelite in my womb to shut me up,

Judah got enraged she answered; He said the object of my anger is directed to you, and your brother Cain, who yoked his accursed seed in your womb to make a god to distroy the holy people on earth because he wanted to be the first to fuck you to make a god as wicked as him.

You are a whore and burdened with the sin of devils to make godly sprits in your flesh, Tamuze shouted its my flesh you lust for and cannot have enough of it, when Elijah cast your ass out of the earth you will miss it, (Jn 8.7; Jer17.1).

Judah restrand himself from hiting her and pushed her away she fell on the floor, Tamuze cried go away satan, murderer, kill me I dont want to bring another god like you on earth, you are vain and decietful, Judah Shouted I am your King and not Elikah, she cried I would rather die than worship a god, he said Elijah dont care about sinners.(Jn8.7)

Tamuze cried its none of your business who I worship, Satan was afraid of Elijah and you want to fight against him. I have to endure your lust, an wickedness for peace, but I will live to see you cry and beg Elijah for peace. She got up from the floor and went to her room and slam the door and began to cry O Elijah have pity on me and save me from this Tyrant.

Elijah spoke in her ears when you are dead, you will see kingdoms from your flesh Created with Sprits of Creation in the time of Salvation. I myself will baptize you before this reprobate and godly sprits from his seed and ask him to repent for his sins before Israelites an godly sprits. Be patient and dont loose faith.

FAITH IN THE ONLY SAVIOUR FOR PEACE

Judah concluded in his anger if he lay his hand on Tamuze he would kill her she would rather die than give up her faith in Elijah, he left the palace went in the harem quater angry, he held Eve and dashed her head on the wall and said, this is for making Cain to be my father to pass on the accursed seed of satan to me not perfect like your people.

Judah said to the pregnant women if any of you fuckers make a god to look like god my father ill slay every one from birth he left the women slamed the door, went on his chariot, hit the horses and sped to Babylon.(Gen6.4)

BEYOND REPROACH (Ps91.16-16 :120.6-7Mt23. !4-15)

Tamuze observed Judah had to prove he could be more wicked than devils, he was zealous for power an did not think much of Elljah and thaught Elijah was another god, took advantage of Elijah's kindness doing the same mistake Cain did not thinking much of Adam not knowing CHRIST was the SPRIT in the body of Adam he could not see. And thaught the devils was superior.

Both Cain and Judah were given the same chioce By CHRIST in the body of Adam and Elijah in the body of god/Cain OBEY to live a long life on earth to rest in Peace for eternity because they are gods born in sin an not accepted in heaven by the Eternal. Both god the father an son made the same mistake an condemned themselves by killing the Sons of CHRIST/ Adam in conspiracy and envie to rule the planet earth.

They did not want Salvation for spritual peace, but conspired with Satan and the devils to hate CHRIST an Elijah who they could not see while they are human. Cain in hades for murder and rape. Judah has commited murder and now abusing his mother, with a plan to declare war against Lord Elijah, the king in the Kingdom and Judge over all sprits on the whole earth. (Jn.21-27:Ps119.16-22:137-142)

THE TEMPLE IN BABYLON

Judah arrived in Babylon and he began to boast to the commandant in his battalion queen tamuze is pregnant for me, I am going to build a temple in the centre of Babylon for every god to come and worship mother an child it will be the begining of my creation to make gods to look like the holy people of Adam we hanged on the tree.

The commandant asked what kind of god will it be? Satan and the devils call us gods because we were born from the flesh of our Hebrew queen Tamuze. Judah said every god Tamuze give birth for me, I will call an Israelite to pass on my seed to make Israelites.

The commandant said, King Judah since we hanged Adam an slay all his sons, I been haveing dreams an in the dreams I see much blood on the earth and Tamuze is always laughing and pointing her finger at satan. In the dream I saw satan an all the devils crying in flames of fire asking Tamuze to tell Elijah to have mercy.

Judah said I am the only king left chosen to rule the nations. Satan an the devils were cowards they had me and battalion of gods to hang an innocent Man, an slay all his SONS to take all their women to make giant gods to populate. Our queen mother is pregnant for me that is why he is crying, because Tamuze is free from him for ever. Now she is rejoiceing with her new king of gods.

Judah continued, comandant I would not like you to be ignorant. Satan an all the devils are removed from living above the earth, they and not returning forever. They are in the fire you saw in your dreams for their wickedness to make gods born in sin in the flesh of Tamuze, so stop worrying what devils will do. Do like me and call your gods a new name so when they pass your seed they will make gods in your name.

The Hebrew women I have in the harem quaters of the palace of satan are all pregnant, I will give you a baby girl from one of the Hebrew women to make a god with you to look like the Man and his kind.

The commandant said, King what name shall I call my kind if I have children with the baby girl you will give me? Judah said, call them mankind so they pass on our godly seed to make mankind and Israelites to populate the earth. Commandant Judah said, techanicaly we are devils after we depart from the flesh of queen Tamuze.

The commandant asked, King Judah you are also the prophet of the law, is it lawful for us to do the same as the devils to make our kind with the holy women you hold in captvity? Judah said it is lawful to change the features of gods to be our new creation in the flesh to worship us as their God, its not important to worship our Hebrew Mother, her Father and Elijah delight in the flesh of gods for Salvation.

The commandant asked; King Judah I know you are a wise king an know hiden secrets of the unknown god who made our queen mother pregant with a god in the palace of Satan. But king Judah we are gods passing on the seed of devil to make gods, all gods look alike, how will we know what is mankind and Israelites?

Judah said, all gods that is speckled we will call mankind what is not speckled like our queen mother will be mine. The commanddant said the gods will hate our queen mother for not giving them children to look like our kind. Judah said I will sell the ones I dont select to our brothers in the market and they will make their kind so all mankind in every generation can mix and mingle with one another to make all kind of features on earth passing on the seed of gods to make their kind of features in their name.

THE BEGINING OF MANKIND AND ISRAELITES

Judah and the commandant with the help of the soldiers started to measure the sight to build the temple for all on earth to come and worship Tamuze and the Israelite son of King Judah

The Temple was built, a Sculptor hewn out of a large stone and sculpted a statue of Tamuze with a son on her arms in the most artful manner portraying queen Tamuze the most beautifull woman for all mankind and Israelites to come in the temlpe to worship mother an child, the statue was placed in the centre of the temple for worshipers to come and worship after she gave birth the first Israelite.

The sculptorers began to make figurings of Tamuze an child for the gods to worship at their homes they calld Tamuze Ishtar goddess of the stars, they called Judah Almighty God out of respect as the only king that was not removed from the earth, the gods swore to worship him for life. They brought special incense in the temple to send up white smoke for the crowd outside to know it was a male Israelite born in Babylon.

THE BIRTH OF THE FIRST ISRAELITE

Tamuze was ready to give birth, she was brought from the palace to the temple. She lay on the altar, the gods began singing and dancing with timbrels, other gods was blowing their trumpet, while others was hand claping saying hail mother of gods give us a son in the name of Israel, others were singing hail queen of storm make a new kind of god for our King to populate the earth like stars in the sky, other gods sang O mother of gods let this Israelite pass on the seed of King Judah like dust on the earth.

The gods kept on, clap, clap mother of gods suffer for our sin dont be silent in this birth let us here you give birth for this Israelite for our king to rejoice with his Israelite.

FEAR OF BIRTH (Ps 58.8.Eccl.1.63Ps58.8Eccl.163)

Tamuze lay on the altar she pushed and pushed but the Israelite would not come out, she became weak and tired she drank water, her legs was trembleing and nervous of what Elijah would do.

Judah became angry, said what is the matter with you? Tamuze cried its afraid you will make it do wickedness on earth, go outside an take your bow and shoot an arrow in the sky for Elijah to see you or kill some badgers to make coats from the skins for your Israelite, It is I who is going to suffer when your Israelite is born for peace on earth. Judah if you dont go out of the temple I will die because of this Israelite.

Judah shouted its Elijah who is making you suffer not me. He an everyone went outside the temlple only the midwife to stay. The midwife said Queen Tamuze take a deep breath and she began to chant O sprit of the unknown god come, Tamuze became afraid an pushed out the Israelite, the Israelite gave out aloud cry in the temple

Judah rushed inside, the others followed and the incense burner sent up the white smoke from the temple for the gods to know queen Tamuze gave birth to a god for the king of gods. The gods outside began to jump with joy, he will be our pope, others said he will be our pastor, others said he will be our witch doctor, others said he will be our rabi with the law in Babylon.

BURNT OFFERING
(Ps 102.3/Heb13.11/Jer6.20Ezek44.11).

The gods outside prepared logs of wood for a burnt offering, then brought big bullock among the bulls of the king and had it to yoke with a white heifer. Then killed the heifer and burnt it on the logs of wood in flames, took the the ashes and put it in a jar for future generations to remember the first Israelite was born in the temple of Babylon.

JESUS KNOWS THE WAY (Ps.1.2-6)

CHRIST was on the throne in heaven meeting Angels from other planets, He asked his Sons where is Jesus? They said He is working on the building project for when our sisters come from earth; CHRIST said go an fetch Jesus for me. Jesus came, said my Father here I am.

CHRIST said, Jesus there is going to be a plague on earth, your your sisters will die, go to earth and wait on the clouds above the nations around Babylon an Elijah will resurrect your Sisters Sprits to you, when they are with you in the cloud, Elijah will say the WORD an you will return on the cloud with your sisters to Me in the tabernacle. Jesus made haste to make his journey to earth and waited in the cloud above the nations.

THE BIRTH OF GIANTS (Joel1.23/Hos.10.13-14)

Judah was in bed with Tamuze, there was much cock crow and wolves howling in the night, the Israelite was crying wanted to be breastfed,

Judah said go an feed the baby, Tamuze said your Israelite is never satisfied his always thirsty for my milk ill get up so I can have peace.

THE REVELATION OF THE MYSTERY PARABLE (LK.8.4-15)

Their was much crying coming from the harem buildings, the women were giving birth, all at the same time, the baby gods were huge and the birth was difficult, all the women died giving birth, the guard rushed in the palace, he said, O king come quickly all the Hebrew women are dead giving birth. The baby gods are crying.

Judah made haste to the harem and saw Eve crying. All my daughters are dead after giving birth to giant baby gods, they need godly women to breast feed them, Judah was in shock seeing dead women and baby gods crying and still in their birth blood.

Judah went back in the palace an said, Tamuze all your sistes in are dead giving birth, Tamuze looked at him in shock, she said can I go and help my Mother with my dead sisters and help her with these baby gods? Judah said no, you cant see them.

Tamuze said, why cant I see my dead sisters? You want me to be an alien to my people even in death. You hanged my Father, slay all my brothers, an now all my Sisters are dead an your Israelite is kicking me in the stomach, what do you want from me she shouted and slamed the door behind her.

Judah rushed inside the room after her in anger, held her throat and said ill kill you if its the last thing I do on this earth. Tamuze said do it now so I can be with my dead sisters, I Have enough of your bitterness an hate for my people.

Judah pushed her away an ran outside the palace puting his head in his hand, realizing his madness wanting to kill his mother, he wanted to cry but tears would not come, abuseing his mother with lust, now he has become a father to crying babies and his mother want him to kill her to join her dead sisters.

JUDAH IS A JEALOUS GOD (Pro 6.6-35/Job33.21)

Judah began talking to himself like a mad man. Tamuze is accepted in heaven and not me, I am consumed with wickedness, malice, hate, deciet, jealousy, an blame Tamuze an god his father for being born in sin an not accepted in heaven an want to destroy all holy people on earth.

Eve became a nursemaid cleaning the baby gods an trying to put order in the place with crying gods, Judah came in the harem with a headach not knowing how to cope with so many gods crying Eve said go quicky an take your soldiers in Babylon an go from house to house an bring godly women with suckling baby gods to breast feed these crying children.

Judah said now I am a god father to giant babies; Eve answered did not Elijah adopt you? Hurry to save the godly childfren before they all die to add to your sin.

Judah took his battalion of soldiers an went from house to house to capture godly women with suckling babies an brought them to the harem to breast feed giant baby gods.

The soldiers took the bodies of the dead women an buried them in a field outside Babylon. Judah locked himself in the dungeon in the palace in fear Elijah would come after him.

The new godly kings an their godly queen mothers from the other nations came to see Judah in fear an breathless. The servants came to see Tamuze an said, queen Tamuze you have guest; She said I am not in the mood to see any one. Your king is in the dungeon tell him he has guest.

Judah came out, Asked the kings, what do you want? The godly queens began to cry, O king of nations all the hebrew women are dead giving birth, their babies are giant godly babies and they are crying, we dont know what to do with them? Also rulers in other tribes we sold some of the Hebrew women came to us an said the women are dead.

The godly queens said; O king dont be angry with us the women did not like our food, an did not have strength to give birth, they complained every day, they didn't like to be living in harems under our kings. Now we have many speckled gods to adopt

Judah was disappointed, his plan to propergate all the women in the haren has failed, only Tamuze is left to make Israelites, Eve is old and past child bearing. Judah said to the kings they must hurry back to their nations an get their soldiers to go in the houses an take the godly women with suckling babies an bring them in their rarem to breast feed the godly giant babies before the the sprits of the Hebrew mothers come an attack us.

In fear of Sprits of the dead women coming to attack them. The godly kings an their qeen mother rushed back to do what Judah said and bury the dead women out side their nation.

Judah did not tell Tamuze her sisters in captivty in the other nations were dead an only she and her Mother is left on earth, he went in the dungeon in the palace to hide in fear of Elijah. (Ezek16.44-45)

THE HOUR FOR RESURECTION HAS COME
(Dan.12:Jn.5.28-29:Mt27.51-53)

Three days after the holy women been buried in the nations. There was lightning, thunder, rain an cloud over the nations, Elijah spoke the WORD in the ear of Eve and Tamuze to look outside.

Jesus was waiting in the cloud. Elijah said, SPIRITS of CHRIST that sleep in the earth awake an arise an go up to the cloud, Jesus is waiting to take you to heaven. The SPRITS of the the dead women awoke from their sleep and started to come out of the graves an began to walk on air going upwards to the cloud to meet Jesus.

NO ONE COMETH TO CHRIST THE FATHER OF SPRITS IN THE LIGHT BUT BY JESUS (Jn.14.6.Jn16.3.Mt6.9

Eve and Tamuze rushed outside and began to see the SPRITS of the dead women walking on air going upwards waving goodbye to them, no god could see this spectacular scene of resurection but the two holy women left on earth Eve an Tamuze.

When all the SPRITS of the women entered in the cloud, their was a flash of lightning in the cloud an Elijah commanded the winds to come upon the cloud an take Jesus an his Sisters to CHRIST on His throne in heaven an Jesus was on his way with his siters to meet CHRIST there Father in the SPRIT for the first time to live the everlasting life forever.

A MAN AN HIS FATHER GO IN THE SAME MAID (Amos2.7Ps137:Ps138)

Judah betroth his Mother, (Tamuze) kept her in captivity like Satan to live by the law, Tamuze became the queen of Babylon. Eve became a nursemaid to supervise the giant babies of her dead daughters while Tamuze gave birth to his Israelites in the palace.

Judah became the God father of gods of the devils, brought up the godly babies to make mankind with different features he selected the best in the harem to mix with his israelites with his mother to propagate an populate, he gave his commandant an soldiers babies of the dead women to make mankind an sold to gods to populate an make all kinds of features. As his creation on earth.

The End of Episode 3.

Followed by episode 4

Episode 3

1. The devils on earth capture all the daughters of CHRIST/Adam and Zion/ Eve
2. The devils rape the daughters of CHRIST/Adam and Zion Eve to make gods and giants on earth.
3. Elijah execute Judgment on Satan and all devils on Earth for rape and send them to Hades to await judgement

Episode 4

1. Mankind
2. The body of Zion/Eve and Jerusalem is burnt on logs of wood by mankind. Elijah saves their Spirit from the flame of fire. The fall of Babylon, The flood on earth, Elijah saves mankind to make kingdoms for salvation to rest in peace after death.

Episode 5

Battle for the earth

1. Final judgment: CHRIST return on the days of salvation to cast out sprits of gods in the kingdom to create Immortal Sprits to continue after salvation. Final Judgment by Elijah and the Spirit of fire to remove sprits of gods that has no rest on Earth to the gate of the sun to put the whole universe in the light with angels by the WORD
2. After Salvation all Spirits in the kingdoms on earth will be immortal perfect as angels in heaven as CHRIST and Zion on the throne in heaven by the WORD to be as it was in the beginning on earth for universal peace and harmony without darkness, Death, devils, and gods on earth forever.